9/11

DESSERTS

FROM THE FAMOUS

LOVELESS CAFE

DESSERTS

FROM THE FAMOUS

LOVELESS CAFE

SIMPLE SOUTHERN PIES, PUDDINGS, CAKES, AND COBBLERS
FROM NASHVILLE'S LANDMARK RESTAURANT

Alisa Huntsman

with contributions by Jim Myers

Foreword by LEE SMITH

ARTISAN

NEW YORK

For mothers, grandmothers, and great-grandmothers:
the bakers who have inspired a lifetime of sweet memories

Copyright © 2011 by Alisa Huntsman and Loveless Cafe, LLC
Photographs copyright © 2011 by Karen Mordechai

Published by Artisan
A division of Workman Publishing Company, Inc.
225 Varick Street
New York, NY 10014-4381
www.artisanbooks.com

Published simultaneously in Canada by Thomas Allen & Son, Limited

Library of Congress Cataloging-in-Publication Data
Huntsman, Alisa.
Desserts from the famous Loveless Cafe : Simple Southern pies, puddings, cakes, and cobblers from
Nashville's landmark restaurant / Alisa Huntsman ; with contributions by Jim Myers ;
foreword by Lee Smith.
p. cm.
Includes bibliographical references and index.
ISBN 978-1-57965-434-4
1. Desserts. 2. Cooking, American—Southern style. 3. Loveless (Cafe) 4. Cookbooks. I. Myers, Jim, 1962–
II. Title.
TX773.H843 2011
641.8'6—dc22   2010051012

Design by Susan E. Baldaserini
Project consultant: Susan Wyler, King Hill Productions

Printed in Singapore
First printing, August 2011

10 9 8 7 6 5 4 3 2 1

CONTENTS

Foreword

Bringing It All Back Home

Writer Thomas Wolfe would never have made his famous statement "You can't go home again" if he'd ever eaten at the Loveless Cafe. Fact is, nothing brings the past back to life as vividly as taste, immediately activating our memories of time, place, circumstance, and who we were then. . . . One bite of the Loveless Cafe's coconut cream pie, for instance, always puts me right back in my mother's southwest Virginia kitchen in about 1963, with Mama in that pretty red-and-white apron with the rickrack ruffles she made herself, pouring her coconut cream pie filling into the crust before she gives me the blue bowl to lick. That filling is the best thing I've ever tasted . . . why, it's the best thing in the world! Mama's smoking a cigarette and drinking coffee with two neighbor ladies as she cooks, and the percolator is perking up some fresh coffee in the corner, while Johnny Cash's new hit "Ring of Fire" blares from the radio on the counter and the coal train roars around the mountain behind the house. Friends, family, community, love . . . it all comes back in one bite of coconut cream pie. I am right there.

    I'll bet you've had this experience yourself at the Loveless, which has the best home cooking this side of heaven. The food just *tastes like home.* Even if your own mama couldn't cook a lick, you still know what home tastes like, don't you? It's an idea, it's an ideal, it's that sweet spot in the center of the heart. We're all home at the Loveless. The trouble is, our own beloved mamas in the rickrack aprons didn't always write their recipes down—at least not with the kind of instructions we need to reproduce them in our own homes. My mother's recipe cards, for instance, often consist of a list of ingredients followed by: "Mix and bake." *Huh?*

Finally, Loveless pastry chef Alisa Huntsman has brought home cooking back home again. Following her careful, clear recipe, I just made a banana pudding to die for. It might even be *better* than Mama's! And let me tell you, if I can do it, you can do it! You don't even have to be Southern. Of Irish and Italian descent herself, Alisa spent years mastering the famous Loveless desserts, then added her own invaluable tricks and tips to come up with this book of gorgeous desserts that really are "Easy as pie!" as she says.

I'm so happy to have this cookbook. Because face it: a meal, even a home-cooked meal, is only a meal—but dessert is always a gift. It's the one gift that I know everybody in my family is going to like. Before I know it, they might even start calling me Mamaw!

—LEE SMITH

Introduction

Just about any list of favorites compiled by road-food devotees includes the Loveless Cafe. In fact, we could hardly be accused of exaggeration if we said the Loveless has become somewhat of an icon in the Southern culinary landscape.

Head out on the stretch of asphalt called Highway 100 that runs southwest from Nashville, and our now-famous neon sign beckons with its promise of hot biscuits and country ham. Indeed, those biscuits have been responsible for our national platform, launching the love of the Loveless into regions far beyond the world of Nashville, Tennessee.

While the Loveless will always be synonymous with biscuits, this book focuses on the bounty of Southern desserts that we serve at the cafe and how you can make them at home. And that presents an interesting story.

Ask any regular who's been coming to the restaurant since its humble beginnings in 1951, when Annie and Lon Loveless started selling fried chicken and biscuits out the front door, and they would have trouble recalling a favorite dessert. As the eponymous motel and cafe grew and changed hands, from the Lovelesses to the Maynards to the McCabes, maybe it was the success of its reputation for chicken, ham, and biscuits that made people forget about dessert altogether. Or maybe some folks came to think of a hot biscuit with melting butter and a spoonful of peach or blackberry preserves as something akin to dessert. But the real story is that the place was so small—only seventy seats—and tables were in such demand that the original owners didn't serve dessert. They felt no need to encourage diners to linger over a cup of coffee and a piece of pie or "nanner" pudding when there were lines of people waiting to fill those tables.

All of that changed soon enough. After years of watching crowds of locals and enlightened travelers stretch the small cafe to its limits and the feet of sated diners wear down the floorboards, the McCabe family decided to sell the property. That could have been the end of the run, but local restaurateur Tom Morales, who had created a name for himself in the movie catering business, stepped in with some other concerned Nashvillians to ensure that the Loveless tradition would continue.

In 2004 the Loveless expanded, and Tom brought me on board just before the big reopening to add desserts to the menu. The renovations to the cafe doubled the seating capacity. We were naïve enough to think all those extra seats would mean that guests would no longer have to queue up for tables like in the old days. How untrue that turned out to be! Folks kept filling up the new space, which meant there were twice as many mouths to feed, and I was there to make sure each one could finish their dinner with something sweet for dessert.

After training at the Culinary Institute of America and working in restaurants in New York City, Washington, D.C., and San Francisco, I came to the Loveless with a love of cakes, a respect for ingredients, a true appreciation for the canon of Southern sweets, and an understanding of people's devotion to them. In anticipation of the big reopening, I was instructed to come up with a banana pudding, a rice pudding, several assorted pies, and a cobbler—typical Southern staples. Easy stuff for an accomplished pastry chef, right? Turns out I had some learning to do.

It's tough to explain the Southern sweet tooth. It might come from a historical access to cane sugar, molasses, and golden sorghum syrup. It might be the instinctual ability to sweeten iced tea right up to the point where one more grain of sugar would cause the pitcher to seize up. When our regulars returned to taste their first piece of pie, they said, "It's good, but it's just not sweet enough." How could that be? I quickly learned that around here, sweeter is better, whether you're talking white sugar, brown sugar, sorghum, molasses, or honey. I suppose it's no accident that one of our best-selling pies, Chess Pie, counts "jess" (just) sugar as its main ingredient. So I tweaked the recipes gradually, notching up the sweetness to please our customers' palates, yet not going overboard. The best recipe testers—then and now—are the waiters and waitresses at the cafe. On any given day, samples of sweets can be found in the break room. Only when a dessert works with the staff does it make it onto our menu at the Loveless.

Southern desserts are a lot like country music, where the complexity of human existence can be distilled into three chords and the truth. It's the same way the clever combination of three simple ingredients like eggs, flour, and sugar can produce something greater than the individual parts. And just like country music, our desserts have a lack of pretension and a simplicity that can be elegant but should never be mistaken for unsophisticated or dull. Above all, our desserts should remind people of home and of the food their mothers or grandmothers used to make.

This cookbook of Southern desserts ensures a degree of immortality for the Loveless and our legacy of feeding hungry folks. When you're too far away to visit us for a bite of our Blueberry Skillet Cobbler or our Double-Coconut Cream Pie, then fall into these pages and get to work. The rate at which you turn out these delicious recipes will be proportional to the number of neighborly drop-in visits you get from friends and family. As you create your own legacy, you'll come to appreciate even more the saying that Southern hospitality begins and ends with dessert.

DESSERTS

FROM THE FAMOUS

LOVELESS CAFE

Blue-Ribbon Pies

Three full pies, clockwise from top left: Peekaboo Blueberry Pie (page 12), Still Holler Blackberry Pie (page 9), and Southern Belle Raspberry Pie (page 29)

You would be hard-pressed to find a decent meat-and-three—that's what we call Southern plate-lunch joints in this part of Tennessee—that doesn't keep a glass cooler up front near the cash register stocked with homemade pies. It's no different at the Loveless. A lot of our customers consider pie to be the cafe's signature dessert, and you see their grins as they take in the full display case, where dense fudge pie competes with coconut cream in a daily popularity contest. And most days, when the lock is turned at the end of service, the only thing the pie cooler holds is empty shelves. Because no matter how full they are when they leave the table, many folks simply cannot resist bringing home a whole pie for later.

Pies are deeply embedded in the South's culinary subconscious. The appeal is universal because, unlike cakes, which can be boastful, pies offer a lesson in sweet and humble happiness. Pie also wins points for being an opportunistic dessert, taking advantage of both pantry staples and seasonal bounty. Our Deep-Dish Spiced Peach Pie and Southern Belle Raspberry Pie are must-haves when fresh fruit is in abundance; yet in the dead of winter you can't go

wrong with our Chess Pie or Turtle Pie, which are made using everyday ingredients.

Even many confident cooks shy away from pie making, and that's a shame. With the step-by-step instructions that lead you along, our crusts are surefire. While most of the recipes in this chapter are designed to work out just fine with a store-bought shell, try the easy made-from-scratch recipes and produce your own tender pie crusts. You'll wonder why you kept that rolling pin hidden for so long.

And don't forget the small portable pastries that tuck nicely in the palm of your hand; hence the name "pickup pies." These simple turnovers, tarts, and free-form galettes hint at spontaneity and are a perfect on-the-go dessert. The only challenge for drivers down middle Tennessee's Highway 100 is that a stop at the Loveless means having to choose from all the delicious pies we serve.

ARKANSAS SWEETLY SPICED APPLE CRUMB PIE

MAKES A 9-INCH PIE; SERVES 6 TO 8

Because the South rarely has freezing nights, which are needed to "set fruit" and develop the flavor and texture that make a really fine apple, we have only a few local varieties to choose from. One is the nearly rock-hard Arkansas Black, named for the darkness of its skin. Of course, in fall our farmers' markets are piled high with red and green apples from our neighbors who enjoy colder climates and mountainous areas. Often at the Loveless, we use Granny Smiths for their pleasing tartness and year-round availability. What makes our apple pie different from others? A single crust, plenty of sweet spices, and a crunchy crumb topping.

9-inch pie shell, unbaked

¾ cup packed light brown sugar

2 tablespoons cornstarch

1 teaspoon ground cinnamon

½ teaspoon freshly grated nutmeg

½ teaspoon ground cardamom

¼ teaspoon ground cloves

6 cups ½-inch-thick sliced peeled apples (1½ to 2 pounds), Arkansas Black, Granny Smith, or any baking variety

Brown Sugar and Oat Crumb Topping (recipe follows)

1. Preheat the oven to 350°F. Place the pie shell on a sturdy baking sheet and set aside.

2. In a large bowl, rub the brown sugar, cornstarch, cinnamon, nutmeg, cardamom, and cloves together with your fingertips until blended. Add the apples and toss to coat. Dump the spiced apple slices into the pie shell, including any sugar and juices that have accumulated in the bowl.

3. Sprinkle the topping evenly over the pie, leaving a 1½-inch border uncovered. (The topping will cover the entire pie. If you put the crumbs close to the edges, they may run out with any juices that boil over, leaving no topping near the edges.)

4. Bake in the middle of the oven for 1 hour and 15 minutes, or until the juices are bubbling and the crumb topping is lightly browned all over. Let cool before cutting, although this is the hardest part, because who can resist warm apple pie?

Brown Sugar and Oat Crumb Topping

MAKES ABOUT 1 CUP

½ cup unbleached all-purpose flour

½ cup rolled oats

⅓ cup packed light brown sugar

½ teaspoon ground cinnamon

⅛ teaspoon baking soda

4 tablespoons cold unsalted butter, cut into small cubes

Place the flour, oats, brown sugar, cinnamon, and baking soda in a bowl and mix gently to break up any lumps of sugar, taking care not to crush the oats. Add the butter and gently rub the ingredients together with your fingertips to produce a mealy mixture with some lumps that clump together when squeezed in your hand.

Baking Tip: The topping can also be prepared by pulsing the ingredients in a food processor, but this cuts the oats and homogenizes the texture. Another method is to use a stand mixer with the paddle attachment, which is the method we use in the cafe to make a large quantity.

STILL HOLLER BLACKBERRY PIE

MAKES A 9-INCH PIE; SERVES 6 TO 8

Blackberries grow all along creeks at the edge of woods, which pretty well describes a country hollow, or "holler." Late July through most of August is the height of fresh blackberry season in Tennessee. When blackberries are not in season, substitute quick-frozen berries, available at the supermarket, which bake up beautifully.

Easy-as-Pie Dough (page 51)

1 cup sugar

3 tablespoons cornstarch

1½ teaspoons grated orange zest

½ teaspoon ground cinnamon

1½ pounds blackberries or marionberries, thawed if frozen (about 3 cups)

2 teaspoons rose water

Baking Tip: Make sure frozen berries are thawed and don't forget to reserve the juices for the filling. The extra time needed to bake only partially thawed fruit can make the difference between a nicely browned pie shell and one that is burned.

1. Preheat the oven to 350°F. Grease a sturdy baking sheet, line it with foil or parchment paper, and grease the liner.

2. To make the bottom shell, roll out one of the dough rounds on a lightly floured surface until a little thicker than ⅛ inch. Fit the pastry into a 9-inch pie pan without stretching it. Trim the pastry all around, leaving a ½-inch overhang. Neatly fold this excess under to double the edge of the crust.

3. Place the sugar, cornstarch, orange zest, and cinnamon in a bowl and rub together with your fingertips to combine. Add the berries and rose water and toss gently to combine. Turn the blackberry filling into the pie shell.

4. To make the top crust, roll out the rest of the dough on a lightly floured surface until a little thicker than ⅛ inch and trim to 10 inches (see photo 1, next page). Roll up ½ to 1 inch of the edge all around to create a raised rim (photo 2). Flute or crimp the raised rim as you would a pie crust (photo 3). Use the wide end of a pastry tip or a very small cutter to remove a 1-inch circle in the middle of the crust.

5. Carefully lift the top and place it in the center of the pie (photo 4). There will be a small gap around the rim, which will allow steam to escape. Set the pie on the lined baking sheet.

continued

Baking Tip: Some of the pie recipes in this chapter call for placing the pie on a sturdy baking sheet lined with greased foil or parchment paper before baking. The baking sheet will catch overflowing juices, the foil or paper will make cleanup easier, and greasing it all prevents the pie dish from sticking to the sheet.

6 Bake in the middle of the oven for 1 hour and 15 minutes, or until the juices are bubbling in the center. Be sure to let cool completely and set before slicing, about 6 hours at room temperature.

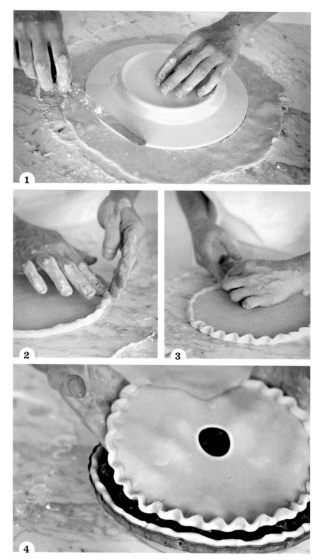

Making a Lattice Top Crust

For simplicity and speed, the lattice crusts on many of the Loveless fruit pies are not actually woven. Instead, wide strips of dough are arranged on top of the pie first in one direction and then in the opposite direction. When the crust bakes, the strips of pastry stick together and form a lovely crisscrossed pattern with the colorful fruit peeking through.

1. To make the lattice top, roll out the Lattice Dough (page 53) or the smaller disk of Flaky Pie Dough (page 48) on a lightly floured surface until ⅛ to ¼ inch thick. With a pizza wheel or a sharp knife, cut the dough into 10 strips about 1 inch wide.

2. Arrange the strips on the pie as follows: Place 1 strip over the center of the pie and 2 strips on either side, leaving about ½ inch in between and trimming to the ends to fit.

3. Then arrange the remaining strips in the opposite direction on a slight diagonal to form a lattice with diamond-shaped openings. Bake as directed in the recipe.

PEEKABOO BLUEBERRY PIE

MAKES A 9-INCH PIE; SERVES 6 TO 8

Blueberries are not native to the South, but newly developed varieties have made the bushes viable for warmer gardening zones, and almost all of our farmers' markets carry them in season. Our customers love the slightly unconventional bite of dried ginger and the floral quality of rose water paired with blueberries.

1½ pounds blueberries
(about 3 cups)

¾ cup sugar

3 tablespoons cornstarch

2 teaspoons grated lemon zest

1 teaspoon ground ginger

1 tablespoon rose water

9-inch pie shell, unbaked

Lattice Dough (page 53)

1. Preheat the oven to 350°F. Rinse the blueberries and pick over to remove any stems or broken fruit. Drain well.

2. In a mixing bowl, rub the sugar, cornstarch, lemon zest, and ginger together with your fingertips. Add the blueberries and rose water and toss gently to combine. Scrape the blueberries with all their sugar and spices into the pie shell.

3. For the top crust, follow the instructions on page 11 to create the lattice. Set the pie on a sturdy baking sheet in the middle of the oven.

4. Bake for 1 hour and 15 minutes, or until the juices are bubbling in the center and the lattice is a light golden brown. Let cool for at least 4 hours to set completely before slicing.

Baking Tip: If you prefer to make the entire crust from scratch, prepare the Flaky Pie Dough (page 48) and use it for both the pie shell and the lattice top.

VARIATION: PEEKABOO TART CHERRY PIE
Substitute 1½ pounds pitted fresh tart cherries for the blueberries (or 3 cups thawed frozen with their juices). Increase the sugar to 1 cup. In place of the ginger and rose water, use ¼ teaspoon ground cinnamon and 1 teaspoon almond extract.

VANILLA BUTTERMILK PIE

MAKES A 9-INCH PIE; SERVES 6 TO 8

There is no substitute for buttermilk in quality baking. It adds a lovely nutty taste, while its natural acidity cuts the gluten in flour, yielding an even more tender texture. The result here is a slightly dense and rich but creamy custard with a bit of a tang, almost like cheesecake. This pie and the Southern staple Chess Pie, which follows, both contain custard fillings, the main difference being that buttermilk pie has a soft, creamy texture and Chess Pie is coarser, fortified as it is with "meal"— white cornmeal to those of you who don't understand Southern speak.

9-inch pie shell, partially baked (see page 49)

1 cup sugar

1 stick (4 ounces) unsalted butter, softened

¼ cup unbleached all-purpose flour

½ vanilla bean, halved lengthwise

3 eggs

1 cup buttermilk

1. Preheat the oven to 350°F. Place the pie shell on a sturdy baking sheet and set aside.

2. In a food processor, combine the sugar, butter, and flour. With the tip of a knife, scrape the vanilla bean seeds into the bowl; reserve the pod for another use. Pulse to combine the mixture. With the machine running, add the eggs, one at a time. Scrape the bowl and, again with the machine on, slowly pour in the buttermilk through the feed tube in a steady stream, mixing just until blended. Pour the buttermilk filling into the pie shell and immediately transfer to the oven.

3. Bake for 40 to 45 minutes, or until the custard is set and a light golden brown across the top. Let cool slightly, then cover and refrigerate until completely cooled and set, 2 to 3 hours. Serve chilled.

Baking Tip: This pie and the Chess Pie and Honey Chess Pie that follow can be made by hand using a mixing bowl and a large wire whisk in place of a food processor. First melt the butter and let it cool completely until opaque and thick but not set. Rub the sugar and vanilla bean seeds together, then whisk into the butter. Whisk in the flour and then the eggs, one at a time, blending well after each addition. Be careful not to add ingredients too quickly. Finally, whisk in the buttermilk a few tablespoons at a time to maintain the emulsion. Pour the filling into the pie shell and bake as directed. The final result will be pretty close in appearance, but a little butter may separate and create a film on top.

CHESS PIE

MAKES A 9-INCH PIE; SERVES 6 TO 8

Chess Pie is a Southern tradition. It's made from simple staples you'll find in any Southern kitchen: sugar, butter, eggs, a little cornmeal for thickening, and a splash of vinegar to balance the sweetness. Many stories attempt to explain the name. The one most prevalent is where the family cook keeps apologizing for her humble recipe, made from a few staple ingredients, by proclaiming that "it's jess pie" . . . "jess" over the years being repeated faster and faster until it became "chess." While this is a real old-timey recipe, it whips up quickly if made the modern way: in a food processor.

9-inch pie shell, partially baked (see page 49)

1⅓ cups sugar

1 stick (4 ounces) unsalted butter, softened

2½ tablespoons white cornmeal

1 teaspoon vanilla extract

4 eggs

½ cup heavy cream

2 tablespoons cider vinegar or distilled white vinegar

1 Preheat the oven to 350°F. Place the pie shell on a sturdy baking sheet and set aside.

2 Place the sugar, butter, cornmeal, and vanilla in a food processor. Run the machine long enough to blend the ingredients completely. Scrape down the sides of the bowl and, with the machine on, add the eggs, one at a time. Scrape down the bowl again and, with the machine running, add the cream through the feed tube in a steady stream; then add the vinegar. Scrape the bowl one last time before processing to blend well. Pour the filling into the pie shell.

3 Bake until the filling is set and golden brown across the top, about 35 minutes. Let cool completely before cutting and serving.

HONEY CHESS PIE

MAKES A 9-INCH PIE; SERVES 8

Some joke that we Southerners have such a sweet tooth, you could just sit us down with a sugar bowl and a spoon and we'd be happy. Most of the recipes in this book take a more subtle approach, but this pie is an exception.

Don't waste your time making this pie with the kind of pasteurized generic honey blends that come in plastic squeeze bottles. Honey is the primary flavor in this pie, and at the cafe, we use an aromatic wildflower variety from a Mennonite community in south-central Kentucky. The honey is such a revelation that it led to the development of this delightfully sweet pie. Think of this dessert when you're at your local farmers' market: Look for a jar of deep golden, freshly harvested nectar.

9-inch pie shell, partially baked (see page 49)

¾ cup wildflower honey

¾ cup packed light brown sugar

1 stick (4 ounces) plus 1 tablespoon unsalted butter, softened

3 tablespoons cornmeal, preferably white

2 tablespoons unbleached all-purpose flour

2 teaspoons vanilla extract

½ teaspoon ground cinnamon

4 eggs, at room temperature

3 tablespoons freshly squeezed lemon juice

⅓ cup heavy cream

1. Preheat the oven to 350°F. Place the pie shell on a sturdy baking sheet and set aside.

2. Place the honey, brown sugar, butter, cornmeal, flour, vanilla, and cinnamon in a food processor. Pulse until the mixture is smooth. With the machine running, add the eggs, one at a time, processing until blended and scraping the bowl after each addition. With the machine on, add the lemon juice and then the heavy cream through the feed tube. Scrape the filling into the pie shell.

3. Bake in the center of the oven for about 40 minutes, or until the edges puff up slightly and the center is firm. Let cool completely before serving.

Baking Tip: Refrigerating this pie will make it easier to cut, but the flavor is best at room temperature. Try chilling the pie thoroughly, cutting neat slices, and letting them stand on their plates for at least half an hour before serving.

DOUBLE-COCONUT CREAM PIE

MAKES A 9-INCH PIE; SERVES 8

Our fudge pie and this coconut cream pie vie for first place in popularity at the Loveless Cafe, with the coconut probably edging out the fudge. Toasting the coconut flakes and using coconut milk in addition to cream make this pie nearly irresistible, as does a thick layer of sweetened whipped cream.

1¼ cups plus 2 tablespoons sweetened shredded coconut

9-inch pie shell, partially baked (see page 49)

2 whole eggs plus 3 egg yolks

1 teaspoon vanilla extract

⅔ cup sugar

⅔ cup canned unsweetened coconut milk

⅔ cup heavy cream

⅔ cup half-and-half

Sweetened Whipped Cream (recipe follows)

1. Preheat the oven to 350°F. Spread out the coconut on a baking sheet and toast in the oven for 5 to 7 minutes, stirring once or twice and watching closely so it doesn't burn, until golden. Transfer the toasted coconut to a plate to cool. Then scatter 1¼ cups of it evenly over the bottom of the partially baked pie shell, reserving the remainder.

2. In a mixing bowl, whisk the whole eggs, the egg yolks, and the vanilla together. Gradually add the sugar and then the coconut milk, mixing until completely blended. Whisk in the heavy cream and half-and-half, but do not beat vigorously or the custard will have bubbles. Gently pour the custard over the coconut in the pie shell and place the pie shell on a sturdy baking sheet.

3. Bake in the middle of the oven for 55 to 60 minutes, until the filling puffs up around the edges and the center is just firm with no shimmy. Remove from the oven and let cool completely, then cover and refrigerate until chilled.

4. Mound the whipped cream on top of the pie, spreading it to the edges in a dome shape. Garnish with the remaining toasted coconut. Serve chilled at once or refrigerate for up to a day.

Sweetened Whipped Cream

MAKES ABOUT 2¾ CUPS

1⅓ cups heavy cream

2 tablespoons sugar

¼ teaspoon vanilla extract

In a chilled mixing bowl with chilled beaters, whip the cream with an electric mixer on medium speed until soft peaks form. Gradually beat in the sugar and vanilla and continue beating until stiff peaks form.

MUDDY FUDGE PIE

MAKES A 9-INCH PIE; SERVES 8

When baking, this pie can go two ways: Take it out when the center still shimmies slightly, and you'll have a creamy, almost puddinglike chocolate pie. Leave it in for another 10 minutes, and the top will puff up, yielding a denser, fudgy pie.

9-inch pie shell, partially baked (see page 49)

3 ounces unsweetened chocolate, chopped

½ cup plus 1 tablespoon half-and-half

½ cup packed light brown sugar

3 eggs

1 cup light corn syrup

1 teaspoon vanilla extract

¼ cup semisweet chocolate chips

Sweetened Whipped Cream (page 19)

1. Preheat the oven to 350°F. Place the partially baked pie shell on a sturdy baking sheet and set aside.

2. In a large microwave-safe bowl, combine the unsweetened chocolate and ½ cup of the half-and-half. On the defrost or low heat setting, microwave for 1 minute. Whisk lightly and then repeat until the mixture is melted and smooth. Make sure the mixture is warmed just enough to melt the chocolate; the hotter this chocolate cream gets, the less creamy the baked pie will be.

3. Place the brown sugar in a separate bowl and break up any lumps. Whisk in the eggs, one at a time, mixing until smooth. Whisk in the corn syrup and vanilla. Gradually whisk about one-quarter of this egg mixture into the chocolate and blend well. It is important to whisk in the eggs slowly and steadily. Continue adding the eggs while whisking until all are combined. Pour the chocolate custard into the pie shell.

4. Bake for about 45 minutes, until the filling is puffy and set around the edges but the center still shimmies. If you want a denser pie, bake for 5 to 10 minutes longer, until it puffs up evenly. Transfer to a wire rack and let cool slightly, then cover and refrigerate until set completely, 3 to 4 hours.

5. To make a chocolate sauce, place the chocolate chips and remaining 1 tablespoon half-and-half in a microwave-safe dish and microwave on low heat until melted, 30 to 60 seconds. Stir until smooth.

6. Mound the whipped cream over the pie, spreading it to the edges. Drizzle the warm chocolate sauce over the whipped cream in a random pattern. Serve at once or refrigerate for up to a day.

ORANGE CREAM PIE

MAKES A 9-INCH PIE; SERVES 6 TO 8

Summer stretches out hot and humid down here in Nashville. That's when we like to turn to cool desserts. With its light, creamy base and refreshing citrus blend of lemon and orange, this chilled pie is reminiscent of a Creamsicle, perfectly suited for hot days. The combination of fresh lemon juice and frozen orange concentrate provides enough intensity to show through the creaminess of the pie.

No-Bake Cookie Crust (page 50), made with graham crackers or gingersnaps

14-ounce can sweetened condensed milk

4 egg yolks

¼ cup plus 2 tablespoons freshly squeezed lemon juice

2 tablespoons thawed orange juice concentrate

1 teaspoon grated orange zest

¾ cup heavy cream

1 tablespoon sugar

⅛ teaspoon vanilla extract

1 Preheat the oven to 350°F. Place the prepared crust on a sturdy baking sheet and set aside.

2 In a mixing bowl, whisk the condensed milk with the egg yolks until well blended. Whisk in the lemon juice, orange juice concentrate, and orange zest until completely mixed. Pour the filling into the crust.

3 Bake for 10 to 15 minutes, just until the custard is hot. The result will be a soft, creamy filling. Let cool slightly, then cover and refrigerate until completely chilled.

4 Shortly before serving, place the cream, sugar, and vanilla in a mixing bowl and whip with an electric mixer on high speed until moderately stiff. Top each slice of pie with a dollop of the whipped cream.

LEMON ICEBOX PIE

You'll find this old-time classic in almost every vintage Southern cookbook, and for good reason: It's easy to make and requires no baking—the original "instant" dessert. Since lemon is the only flavor used and the juice is what "bakes" the pie, be sure to use the freshest lemons you can find.

14-ounce can sweetened condensed milk

3 fresh egg yolks, preferably organic

½ cup freshly squeezed lemon juice (3 to 4 lemons)

1 tablespoon grated lemon zest

No-Bake Cookie Crust (page 50), made with gingersnaps or vanilla wafers, or a 9-inch store-bought cookie crumb crust

1 cup heavy cream

1½ tablespoons sugar

¼ teaspoon vanilla extract

1. Place the condensed milk in a medium bowl and whisk in the egg yolks until completely combined. Whisk in the lemon juice and zest. Pour the lemon filling into the prepared crust.

2. Press a sheet of plastic wrap directly onto the surface and refrigerate for at least 8 hours, preferably overnight.

3. Shortly before serving, place the cream, sugar, and vanilla in a mixing bowl and whip with an electric mixer on high speed until moderately stiff. Spread the whipped cream evenly over the top of the pie.

Baking Tip: This pie is a no-bake recipe, which contains raw egg yolks. This may not be a problem if you have a reliable source for very fresh, organic eggs. However, to practice caution, especially if anyone eating the pie is pregnant or otherwise sensitive, you can bake it in a 350°F oven for 10 to 15 minutes, just until the yolks are warmed to at least 140°F and set. Then let cool and refrigerate until chilled.

OUT-OF-THE-PAN PEACH PIE

MAKES 2 SMALL FLAT PIES, ABOUT 7 INCHES IN DIAMETER; SERVES 4 TO 6

Lightly sweetened ripe peaches are heaped on a round of dough set right on the baking sheet. The edges of the pastry are folded over, leaving most of the fruit visible in the center, like a French galette. Omitting the pan means you don't have to worry about fitting, tearing, or crimping the pastry. This pie is best still warm from the oven, served with a scoop of butter pecan ice cream.

4 cups fresh peach slices, peeled or not (2½ to 3 pounds fresh peaches)

¼ cup plus 2 tablespoons granulated sugar

¼ cup unbleached all-purpose flour

1 teaspoon pumpkin pie spice

½ recipe Easy-as-Pie Dough (page 51)

Egg wash: 1 egg, beaten with 1 tablespoon water

2 tablespoons coarse sugar

1. Preheat the oven to 350°F. Line 2 sturdy baking sheets with parchment paper and lightly grease the paper.

2. In a medium bowl, toss the peaches with the granulated sugar, flour, and pumpkin pie spice.

3. Divide the dough into two pieces and roll out one piece on a lightly floured board or parchment paper into a 10-inch circle. Carefully invert the dough onto one of the lined baking sheets. Scoop 2 cups of the peach filling into a mound in the center of the circle of dough, leaving a 1½- to 2-inch margin all around. Fold the edges of the dough in toward the center, pleating as necessary; do this all the way around so that the peaches are visible in the middle.

4. Brush the edges of the pastry with egg wash and sprinkle with 1 tablespoon of the coarse sugar. Repeat with the remaining dough, peach filling, egg wash, and coarse sugar.

5. Bake for about 20 minutes, or until the crust is golden brown and the juices are bubbling.

DEEP-DISH SPICED PEACH PIE

MAKES A 9-INCH PIE; SERVES 6 TO 8

Pumpkin pie spice is basically cinnamon, allspice, nutmeg, ginger, and cloves—and some also includes coriander. While this traditional Yankee blend sounds as if it would overwhelm the delicacy of the peaches, it only enhances their flavor. And cardamom, with its crisp licorice overtones, is a spice that complements many fruits. Serve this pie plain or with a scoop of peach or vanilla ice cream.

9-inch deep-dish pie shell, unbaked

¾ cup sugar

3 tablespoons cornstarch

2 teaspoons grated lemon zest

Seeds from ¼ vanilla bean or 1 teaspoon vanilla extract

1½ teaspoons pumpkin pie spice

½ teaspoon ground cardamom

4 cups sliced peeled peaches (2½ to 3 pounds fresh peaches)

Lattice Dough (page 53)

1. Preheat the oven to 350°F. Grease a sturdy baking sheet, line it with foil or parchment paper, and grease the liner. Place the pie shell on the baking sheet and set aside.

2. In a bowl, combine the sugar, cornstarch, lemon zest, vanilla seeds, pumpkin pie spice, and cardamom. Rub together with your fingertips to mix thoroughly. Add the peaches and toss to coat them well. Scrape the fruit and any juices and seasonings into the pie shell.

3. For the top crust, make the Lattice Dough. Roll out, cut into 1-inch-wide strips, and arrange in a lattice on top, as illustrated on page 11.

4. Bake for 1 hour and 15 minutes, or until the juices are bubbling gently in the center and the lattice crust is golden brown. Let cool completely to set the filling before cutting. Serve slightly warm or at room temperature.

Baking Tip: If you prefer to make the entire pie crust from scratch, prepare the Flaky Pie Dough (page 48) and use it for both the shell and the lattice top.

PERSIMMON PIE

MAKES A 9-INCH PIE; SERVES 6 TO 8

Southern persimmons look very different from the big red Italian beauties often seen in the North, or even from the paler, Japanese-style Hachiya persimmons most commonly carried by supermarkets. Our persimmons are small, only slightly larger than a cherry. When ripe, they turn a deep pumpkin-orange color and develop an intense, almost datelike flavor.

The persimmon tree has a long history in Tennessee, where the original inhabitants, the Cherokee, were skilled at cultivating the fruit. The trees are sensitive to even the smallest changes in weather, which is why we always keep some puree, made from freshly harvested fruit, in the freezer. To make the puree, gather the fruits after the first frost, which is when they will be sweetest, wash them well, and run them through the fine blade of an old-fashioned food mill to extract the pulp while removing the skins and the seeds.

9-inch pie shell, partially baked (see page 49)

1 cup persimmon puree (about 4 cups small Southern persimmons or 4 to 6 Italian or Japanese persimmons)

2/3 cup packed dark brown sugar

3/4 teaspoon ground cinnamon

1/2 teaspoon freshly grated nutmeg

2 eggs

1/2 cup heavy cream

Whipped cream (optional)

1 Preheat the oven to 350°F. Place the pie shell on a sturdy baking sheet and set aside.

2 In a mixing bowl, whisk the persimmon puree, brown sugar, cinnamon, and nutmeg together. Whisk in the eggs, one at a time, and then the heavy cream. Pour the persimmon filling into the pie shell.

3 Bake for 30 minutes, or until just set. Let the pie cool completely before cutting. Serve plain or with a dollop of whipped cream, if desired.

SOUTHERN BELLE RASPBERRY PIE

MAKES A 9-INCH PIE; SERVES 8

Nothing is as intense as raspberry pie. Or as jewel-like in color or, it turns out, as easy to make. This version adds a citrusy floral undertone with orange zest and rose water, the kind Southern belles used to dab at their temples in the heat.

Since this country pie uses a generous amount of berries, don't apologize if you resort to frozen. Just choose unsweetened, individually quick-frozen raspberries. Measure the fruit while frozen and thaw thoroughly before using. Serve plain or with a small scoop of chocolate or orange sorbet.

9-inch prepared pie shell, unbaked

¾ cup sugar

¼ cup cornstarch

2 teaspoons grated orange zest

2 teaspoons rose water

½ vanilla bean, split lengthwise in half

1½ pounds fresh raspberries (5 to 6 cups)

Lattice Dough (page 53)

1. Preheat the oven to 350°F. Line a sturdy baking sheet with parchment paper and lightly grease the paper. Place the pie shell on the baking sheet and set aside.

2. In a mixing bowl, combine the sugar, cornstarch, orange zest, and rose water. With the tip of a small knife, scrape the seeds from the vanilla bean into the bowl. Rub the ingredients together with your fingertips to combine them. Add the raspberries and toss to coat. Turn them into the pie shell.

3. For the top crust, make the Lattice Dough. Roll out, cut into 1-inch-wide strips, and arrange in a lattice on top, as illustrated on page 11.

4. Bake for 1 hour and 15 minutes, or until the juices are bubbling in the center and the lattice top is golden brown. Let cool and set for at least 4 to 6 hours, or the filling will be runny when the pie is cut. Serve at room temperature.

Baking Tip: If you prefer to make the entire pie crust from scratch, prepare the Flaky Pie Dough (page 48) and use it for both the shell and the lattice top.

STRAWBERRY RHUBARB PIE

MAKES A 9-INCH PIE; SERVES 6 TO 8

In Tennessee, strawberries and rhubarb are ready to harvest by late spring or early summer, depending on the varieties, and they stop producing when the high heat of summer sets in. Since they grow together, they are often paired and make a great pie. Our version is also embellished with extra spices and grated orange zest. Serve plain or with a scoop of buttermilk ice cream.

9-inch prepared pie shell, unbaked

1 cup sugar

3 tablespoons cornstarch

1½ teaspoons grated orange zest

1 teaspoon apple pie spice

1 teaspoon ground cinnamon

12 ounces fresh strawberries, hulled and halved (about 2 cups)

12 ounces fresh rhubarb, cut into ½-inch slices (about 2 cups)

Lattice Dough (page 53)

1. Preheat the oven to 350°F. Grease a sturdy baking sheet, line it with parchment paper or foil, and grease the liner. Place the pie shell on the baking sheet and set aside.

2. In a bowl, rub the sugar, cornstarch, orange zest, apple pie spice, and cinnamon together with your fingertips. Add the strawberries and rhubarb, toss together gently with a rubber spatula, and turn the fruit into the pie shell, using the spatula to scrape the bowl well.

3. For the top crust, make the Lattice Dough. Roll out, cut into 1-inch-wide strips, and arrange in a lattice on top, as illustrated on page 11.

4. Bake for about 1 hour and 15 minutes, or until the juices are bubbling in the center and the lattice is a nice golden brown.

Baking Tip: If you prefer to make the entire pie crust from scratch, prepare the Flaky Pie Dough (page 48) and use it for both the shell and the lattice top.

Tips for Easy Pie Shells

The desserts in this book are billed as being "simple Southern." That's why some of the recipes don't demand homemade pastry: When a recipe calls for just a "pie shell," you can with all good conscience use a quality store-bought pastry shell. Prepared refrigerated or thawed frozen pastry shells work especially well in these recipes because so many of the pies are single crust, filled and baked shortly before serving. If, however, you prefer to make the entire crust from scratch, try the Flaky Pie Dough (page 48). For a lattice-top pie, you can use about two-thirds for the shell and the remainder for the lattice top.

Another option when a lattice top is involved, as in the Peekaboo Blueberry Pie (page 12) and the Deep-Dish Spiced Peach Pie (page 26), is to purchase a prepared shell and just make the Lattice Dough (page 53) for the top; it was developed specifically for this purpose. Because Lattice Dough contains egg yolk and confectioners' sugar in addition to flour and butter, its texture is more like that of a cookie dough, which is very easy to work with and needs no glaze.

TENNESSEE SWEET POTATO PIE

MAKES A 9-INCH PIE; SERVES 6 TO 8

Choose a sweet potato with sweet bright yellow or orange flesh for this pie. At the Loveless, most of our sweet potatoes are giants that come from Mississippi. The smoother the sweet potato puree, the creamier and more attractive the pie; so after cooking thoroughly, be sure to mash them well or use a food mill, ricer, or food processor to do the job. Sorghum is a deep amber syrup familiar to those who live in the South, especially Tennessee and Alabama, exotic to those who don't. For this pie, sorghum and honey are really interchangeable. Do not, however, substitute molasses; it is too strongly flavored.

2 to 3 medium-large sweet potatoes, about 1½ pounds

9-inch pie shell, partially baked (see page 49)

2 tablespoons unsalted butter, melted

⅓ cup packed dark brown sugar

3 tablespoons sorghum or wildflower honey

¾ teaspoon ground cinnamon

½ teaspoon freshly grated nutmeg

3 eggs

½ cup heavy cream

Whipped cream or sorghum (optional)

1. Preheat the oven to 375°F. Place the sweet potatoes in an ovenproof dish and bake for 45 minutes, until very soft. When cool enough to handle, peel off the skins and mash the flesh well so there are no lumps. Measure out 2 cups and let stand until tepid.

2. Reduce the oven temperature to 350°F. Set the pie shell on a sturdy baking sheet.

3. In a large bowl, whisk the sweet potatoes and melted butter together. Gradually whisk in the brown sugar. Add the sorghum, cinnamon, and nutmeg; mix well. Whisk in the eggs, one at a time, mixing well and scraping down the sides of the bowl between additions. Blend in the cream. Scrape the sweet potato filling into the pie shell.

4. Bake for 45 to 50 minutes, or until the edges are puffed and the center is almost firm but still flat. Let cool completely before serving. Garnish with whipped cream or a drizzle of sorghum, if desired.

CHOCOLATE COOKIE–PEANUT BUTTER PIE

MAKES A 9-INCH PIE; SERVES 8

This is one pie that is always on the menu. Peanut butter is hugely popular in the South, and pairing it with chocolate creates a dessert that appeals to everyone. Of course, ours is special, served in a crunchy homemade chocolate cookie crust.

No-Bake Cookie Crust (page 50), made with chocolate wafer cookies

½ cup packed light brown sugar

¾ cup light corn syrup

½ cup half-and-half

½ cup smooth peanut butter, at room temperature

1 teaspoon vanilla extract

3 eggs

Whipped cream and chopped peanuts, for topping

1 Preheat the oven to 350°F. Place the prepared crust on a sturdy baking sheet and set aside.

2 In a large mixing bowl, use your fingertips to break up any lumps in the brown sugar. Add the corn syrup, half-and-half, peanut butter, and vanilla. Using a whisk, mix the ingredients until smooth and completely combined. Whisk in the eggs and scrape the filling into the pie crust.

3 Bake for 40 to 45 minutes, until the edges are puffed and set but the center of the pie appears soft and shimmies slightly. Let the pie cool completely before topping with whipped cream and a sprinkling of chopped peanuts.

Baking Tip: Use a commercial homogenized peanut butter for this recipe. "Natural" or freshly ground peanut butter will not work well here.

Chocolate Cookie–Peanut Butter Pie (left) and Turtle Pie (right, page 37)

Melting Chocolate

Chocolate scorches if allowed to heat above 120°F. Even if you are careful, melting it over direct heat can easily cause burns in spots. Chocolate also "seizes"—becomes grainy and tough—if it comes in contact with even a few drops of water. For these reasons, a double boiler is ideal for melting chocolate, because water in the bottom container tempers the heat of the stove while the top container shields the chocolate from any moisture. If you don't have a double boiler, set a stainless-steel mixing bowl over, not directly touching, a pan of water that is just below a simmer over low heat. The warm bowl keeps the melted chocolate fluid while you add other ingredients and make your batter or frosting.

A microwave is not as reliable for melting because the heat is very uneven and power varies from model to model, making it easy to burn the chocolate in spots. That said, we recommend using a microwave for melting either very small amounts of chocolate or larger quantities with a substantial amount of liquid, such as cream or half-and-half. Place the chocolate and liquid, if using, in a microwave-safe bowl and heat on the lowest setting or the defrost setting for 30 seconds for very small amounts (2 ounces or less) or 45 to 60 seconds for larger amounts; stir well. Microwave for 30 seconds and stir again. Repeat, if necessary, until the mixture is melted, shiny, and satiny smooth.

TURTLE PIE

MAKES A 9-INCH PIE; SERVES 8 TO 10

Some might debate whether this dessert is a pastry or a confection, but either way, at the Loveless this pie disappears as quickly as we make it. While the recipe is really easy to prepare, do allow a little extra time because you're going to be "baking" your own caramel.

Two 14-ounce cans sweetened condensed milk

No-Bake Cookie Crust (page 50), made with chocolate wafer cookies

8 ounces semisweet chocolate chips or a chopped bar

½ cup half-and-half

¼ cup pecan pieces

1 Preheat the oven to 350°F.

2 Pour the condensed milk into a glass or ceramic 1½- to 2-quart ovenproof dish at least 2 inches deep. Cover the dish with foil and set it in a roasting pan. Pour enough hot water into the roasting pan to reach the same level as the milk. Place the pans in the center of the oven and bake for about 2 hours, carefully folding back the foil and stirring the condensed milk every 15 to 20 minutes. Scrape the sides and bottom of the dish well to prevent scorching. When the caramel is a rich amber color, carefully remove the dish from the pan of water and set it on a towel to dry off. Pour the hot caramel into the crust, wrap with plastic, and refrigerate until cold and set, about 6 hours or overnight.

3 To make the chocolate topping, place the chocolate and half-and-half in the top of a double boiler or in a heatproof bowl. Set over (not in) barely simmering water over low heat and warm, stirring occasionally, until the chocolate is melted. Remove from the heat and whisk until smooth. Or follow the microwave directions opposite.

4 Pour the chocolate cream over the chilled caramel in the pie, spreading it evenly to cover. Sprinkle the pecans over the top and return the pie to the refrigerator until the chocolate sets, about 30 minutes. The best way to cut this pie is to use a knife that has been dipped in hot water, dipping and wiping the blade between slices.

Photograph on page 35.

LOVELESS STEEPLECHASE PIE

MAKES A 9-INCH PIE; SERVES 8

The exciting Iroquois Steeplechase is a breathtaking three-mile race held in Nashville the second Saturday in May, a week after the Kentucky Derby. Since the folks in Louisville have their own signature Derby Pie, we decided our Loveless customers should have one too. So we added our world-famous Tennessee sippin' whiskey and chocolate chips to pecan pie, and our Steeplechase Pie was born. During race week, every single slice sells. It doesn't do too badly when we slip it onto the dessert menus the rest of the year either.

1¼ cups pecan pieces

½ cup semisweet chocolate chips

9-inch pie shell, partially baked (see page 49)

¾ cup sugar

6 tablespoons unsalted butter, melted

2 tablespoons Tennessee whiskey, such as Jack Daniel's

1 teaspoon vanilla extract

3 eggs

¾ cup light corn syrup

1 Preheat the oven to 350°F. Toss the pecans with the chocolate chips and scatter them evenly over the bottom of the pie shell.

2 Put the sugar in a mixing bowl; add the melted butter, whiskey, and vanilla and whisk to combine. Add the eggs, one at a time, mixing well after each addition. Add the corn syrup and whisk until blended. Pour this mixture over the nuts and chips in the pie shell.

3 Set the pie on a sturdy baking sheet in the middle of the oven. Bake for 50 to 55 minutes, until the filling puffs up a bit and is set across the top of the pie. Let cool completely before cutting.

Pickup Pies

When appropriate, we like to eat with our fingers in the South—think of ribs, fried chicken, barbecue. . . . Well, dessert is no exception. Our pickup pies range from traditional baked turnovers to "naked pies," rustic fruit pastries very much like miniature galettes. Both types are made without a pie pan. What they also share are their size and simplicity. Though they are fine eaten out of hand, at the cafe we serve them on plates with a fork, sometimes accompanied by whipped cream or ice cream.

APPLE TURNOVERS

MAKES 8 LARGE TURNOVERS

These flaky pastries filled with cinnamony-sweet apples are irresistible as well as quick and easy to make. Serve them while they are still warm.

Two 10-inch-square sheets store-bought puff pastry, thawed if frozen

2½ cups diced peeled apples (2 to 3 large apples)

⅓ cup sugar, plus more for sprinkling

2 tablespoons unbleached all-purpose flour

½ teaspoon ground cinnamon

Egg wash: 1 egg, beaten with 1 tablespoon water

1   Preheat the oven to 400°F. Line a large baking sheet with parchment paper and grease the paper.

2   Lay the puff pastry out on a flat surface and cut each sheet into four 5-inch squares.

3   Toss the diced apples with the ⅓ cup sugar, the flour, and the cinnamon. Continue to mix until the moisture causes the sugar mixture to adhere to the apples. Divide the filling among the turnovers, spooning it closer to one corner. Brush the 2 edges of dough closest to the filling with egg wash. Fold over to form a triangle that covers the filling and press the edges together to seal. Place the turnovers on the baking sheet, brush the tops lightly with more of the egg wash, and dust with some additional sugar.

4   Bake for 20 to 25 minutes, until they are puffed, the tops are golden brown, and the folded edge no longer looks translucent. Be sure to let cool for at least 10 minutes before serving; the enclosed filling gets very hot! Serve warm or at room temperature.

VARIATION: GINGERED PEACH TURNOVERS

Prepare the turnovers as described, substituting diced peeled peaches for the apples. Substitute ¼ cup packed dark brown sugar for the ⅓ cup sugar, add ½ teaspoon ground ginger to the cinnamon, and sprinkle the top of the turnovers with coarse sugar before baking.

NAKED BERRY PIES

"Naked" here refers to the lack of a pie pan. These individual berry pies are formed right on the baking sheet without any fussy fitting or crimping. Each person gets not just a slice but a whole little pie. Berries are simply mounded on circles of dough on a baking sheet, and the edges are folded up and over to form a wide edge, much like a French galette. These pies bake in less than half an hour, and it takes only two cups of berries to serve four people, or more if you decide to share. They offer the perfect finish to a big country breakfast or brunch.

½ recipe Easy-as-Pie Dough (page 51)

2 cups raspberries, blueberries, blackberries, or a mixture

⅓ cup granulated sugar

3 tablespoons unbleached all-purpose flour

1 teaspoon grated orange zest

1 teaspoon vanilla extract

½ teaspoon ground cardamom

Egg wash: 1 egg, beaten with 1 tablespoon water

Coarse sugar

1 Preheat the oven to 375°F. Line 2 sturdy baking sheets with parchment paper or foil and grease the liners lightly. Divide the dough into 4 equal pieces and roll each out to an 8-inch circle. Arrange the dough circles on the baking sheets.

2 Just before you're ready to bake, place the berries in a medium bowl. Add the granulated sugar, flour, orange zest, vanilla, and cardamom and toss gently until the berries are coated. Immediately spoon a heaping ½ cup of berries onto the middle of each dough circle. Fold the edges in toward the center, pleating the dough as necessary and leaving at least a 2-inch circle of fruit exposed. Brush the crust with egg wash and sprinkle coarse sugar evenly over the tops.

3 Bake for 25 minutes, or until the juices are bubbling. Let cool for at least 15 minutes before serving to allow the juices to thicken.

LEMON MERINGUE PIE-LETS

MAKES 8 INDIVIDUAL PIES

Certainly you've heard of tartlets? Well, these are pie-lets—little lemon pies with clouds of fluffy meringue billowing on top. Save yourself the work of forming eight individual shells by purchasing miniature pie shells, which are available in the frozen food section of the supermarket. All you have to do is make the lemon pie filling and meringue, assemble, and bake.

8 store-bought individual pie shells, about 3 inches in diameter, baked according to the instructions on the package and cooled

Lemon Pie Filling (recipe follows) or 2 cups store-bought lemon curd

4 egg whites

¼ teaspoon cream of tartar

½ cup sugar

1 Preheat the oven to 350°F. Fill each baked pie shell with about ¼ cup chilled lemon pie filling.

2 In a large mixing bowl, whip the egg whites with the cream of tartar until they are foamy. Very gradually beat in the sugar. Continue to whip until stiff peaks form; the tops should droop slightly when the beater is lifted. Do not overbeat, or the meringue will lose volume when it bakes.

3 Using a large spoon, dollop the meringue over each pie. With the back of the spoon, spread the meringue to the edges, covering the filling completely and leaving a dome in the center. Touch the back of the spoon to the meringue and pull up quickly to make little spikes.

4 Place the pies on a sturdy baking sheet and bake for 10 to 15 minutes, until the tips of the spikes are a nice golden brown. Remove from the oven and serve immediately.

Lemon Pie Filling

MAKES ABOUT 2 CUPS

1 cup sugar

3 tablespoons cornstarch

1 cup lemon juice, preferably fresh squeezed (5 to 6 lemons)

6 egg yolks

2 tablespoons unsalted butter, softened

Grated zest of 1 lemon

1 In a small, heavy nonreactive saucepan, whisk the sugar and cornstarch together. Whisk in the lemon juice until smooth. Then add the egg yolks and whisk until well blended. Set over medium heat and cook, whisking constantly, until the mixture comes to a slow boil, 5 to 7 minutes.

2 Reduce the heat slightly and boil for 1 full minute to cook the cornstarch. Strain the lemon filling into a heatproof glass or ceramic bowl. Add the butter and whisk until melted and smooth. Whisk in the lemon zest. Press a sheet of plastic wrap directly onto the top to prevent a skin from forming and refrigerate until the filling is cold.

Baking Tips

• Most of us are taught never to boil egg yolks lest they curdle. Well, that's true, except when you combine them with a starch, like flour or the cornstarch used here, which stabilizes the eggs so they can be cooked through yet remain smooth and silky.

• Lemon Pie Filling can be made up to 3 days in advance. Store it in a glass, plastic, or ceramic container in the refrigerator.

• If you do not want to squeeze so many lemons, buy the lemon juice found in the freezer section rather than the stuff in the big green bottles or the little plastic lemons. It's a much fresher-tasting product. Then you need to purchase only one lemon, for the zest.

PEAR PICKUP PIES

MAKES 6 INDIVIDUAL PIES

Any variety of pear can be used for this recipe, but we use Anjou because they tend to hold their shape. Cardamom combined with lemon and cinnamon works magic with pears.

2 medium-large ripe pears (about 1 pound)

⅓ cup granulated sugar

2 tablespoons unbleached all-purpose flour

1 teaspoon grated lemon zest

½ teaspoon ground cinnamon

¼ teaspoon ground cardamom

½ recipe Easy-as-Pie Dough (page 51)

Egg wash: 1 egg, beaten with 1 tablespoon water

Coarse sugar

1. Preheat the oven to 375°F. Line 2 sturdy baking sheets with parchment paper and grease the paper.

2. Peel the pears and cut them into quarters. (The recipe requires only 6 pieces, so be sure to eat the other two before proceeding with the recipe.) Remove the stems and cores, then slice each quarter lengthwise starting 1 inch from the stem end to the bottom every ¼ inch. Using gentle pressure, flatten the cuts to form a fan. The uncut stem end should hold the slices together and make them easier to handle.

3. Combine the granulated sugar, flour, lemon zest, cinnamon, and cardamom in a small bowl and rub together with your fingers. Set the spiced sugar aside.

4. Divide the dough into 6 pieces and shape each one into a small round patty. On a floured board, roll out each piece of dough into a 7-inch round a little more than ⅛ inch thick. Arrange them on the lined baking sheets. Sprinkle a heaping tablespoon of the spiced sugar over each pastry round, leaving a 1-inch margin around the edge. Top with a pear fan and fold the edges in toward the center, pleating as necessary, leaving the fruit exposed in the center. Brush the egg wash over the pastry edges and sprinkle the coarse sugar over the pies.

5. Bake for about 15 minutes, until the dough is golden brown and the juices begin to bubble. Let cool for at least 10 minutes before serving.

Pie Doughs and Crusts

Many otherwise confident home bakers are afraid of making pie crust. Have no fear: this section contains several reliable pastry recipes along with an easy technique for partially baking a pie shell—whether homemade or store-bought—which is used in many of the single-crust pies in this chapter. In addition to a No-Bake Cookie Crust, an all-purpose Flaky Pie Dough, and a sweetened Easy-as-Pie Dough, there's a Lattice Dough, perfect for creating lattice tops just like we do on the fruit pies at the Loveless. It makes a small quantity and is very forgiving, with no need for an egg wash or glaze. It also gives you the option of using a prepared refrigerated or frozen pie shell for the bottom to make baking a pie even easier.

FLAKY PIE DOUGH

MAKES ENOUGH DOUGH FOR 1 DOUBLE-CRUST 9-INCH PIE, 2 SINGLE-CRUST
9-INCH PIES, OR A 9-INCH PIE COVERED WITH A LATTICE TOP

If you want to make your own pastry, this buttery, tender dough is the recipe to use.

1/3 cup cold water

1½ tablespoons distilled
white vinegar

2⅔ cups unbleached
all-purpose flour

1¼ teaspoons salt

2 sticks (8 ounces) cold
unsalted butter, cut into
small cubes

Baking Tips

• The more you work pie dough,
the tougher it gets, so try not
to reroll the dough. This is
especially true for lattice tops.
By working with a portion
of the dough at a time and
rolling it into rectangles, you
will eliminate the need to use
the scraps.

• If you are making only one
single-crust pie, wrap and
freeze the other piece of
dough for later use. It will keep
well in the freezer for up to
2 months.

1 Combine the water and vinegar in a cup and refrigerate while
you begin the dough.

2 Place the flour and salt in a mixing bowl and stir to combine.
Add the butter and toss to coat with the flour, making sure the
small cubes are separated. Using your fingertips, a fork, or a
pastry blender, cut the butter into the flour until some bits are
the size of peppercorns and others the size of peas. Sprinkle
the cold water and vinegar mixture over the dough while
tossing with a fork to moisten evenly. If the dough is crumbly
or has pockets of dry ingredients, add a little more cold water
until it is moistened and pliable but not sticky.

3 For a double-crust pie, pat one-third of the dough into a
4-inch disk for the top crust and the remaining dough into a
larger disk for the bottom crust; wrap and chill for at least
30 minutes before using.

4 For a lattice-top pie, follow the same guidelines, but when
rolling out the smaller disk of dough, do it in two batches so
that the second half remains firm and easy to handle. Roll
the dough into rectangles that are slightly longer than the
diameter of the pie. For single-crust pies, simply divide the
dough into two equal pieces to roll out as needed.

How to Make a
Partially Baked Pie Shell

This technique is for a pie shell you've made yourself or a frozen or refrigerated crust you've purchased. The time and temperature called for here result in what is technically a "blind-baked shell," cooked just enough to hold a filling without turning soggy and to allow further baking without darkening the rim.

1. If using homemade Flaky Pie Dough (opposite), roll out one disk of dough on a lightly floured surface to a round $1/16$ to $1/8$ inch thick. Carefully fold into quarters or wrap over the rolling pin and transfer to a 9-inch pie plate. Ease the dough into the pan without stretching. Trim the edges to leave an overhang of about $1/2$ inch. Fold under and crimp decoratively. Refrigerate the pie shell while the oven heats.

2. Preheat the oven to 325°F. Whether using a store-bought prepared shell or homemade pastry, place the pie shell on a sturdy baking sheet to make it easier to maneuver. Line the pie shell with parchment paper and fill with 3 cups dried beans or pie weights.

3. Bake the pie shell for 18 to 20 minutes. The dough should look fairly dry but not at all browned. Remove from the oven. Using a large spoon, scoop out the beans or pie weights. Remove the paper and let the shell cool completely before proceeding with your recipe. Be sure to save the beans; they can be reused many times.

Baking Tip: If you have trouble handling dough successfully, try rolling out the disk on a floured sheet of parchment paper or wax paper. Then you can just lift the paper and invert the dough into the pie dish.

NO-BAKE COOKIE CRUST

MAKES A 9-INCH PIE SHELL

The best cookies to use for this crust are those with a lower fat content. Depending on the flavor you want, some suggestions include biscotti (but *not* those that have been dipped in chocolate), gingersnaps, graham crackers, and chocolate wafers. Higher-fat butter cookies will produce a looser, oilier crust without the pleasing crisp texture you want.

1 cup cookie crumbs

2 tablespoons sugar

1 tablespoon very finely chopped nuts (optional)

3 tablespoons unsalted butter, melted

Place the cookie crumbs, sugar, and nuts, if using, in a bowl and stir to mix. Add the melted butter and toss with a fork until evenly moistened. Pour into a 9-inch pie pan. Using your fingertips, pat the mixture evenly across the bottom and up the sides of the pan, pressing gently to pack it.

Baking Tips

• Work quickly while the butter is still warm and liquid; the crumbs will be much easier to manipulate. Once the butter chills and sets, it's almost impossible to shape a smooth, even crust.

• This easy pie shell can be stored in the refrigerator for up to a week or wrapped well and frozen for up to 2 months.

EASY-AS-PIE DOUGH

MAKES ENOUGH DOUGH FOR 1 DOUBLE-CRUST 9-INCH PIE OR
2 SINGLE-CRUST PIES, OR 12 SMALLER PICKUP PIES

Because of the large amount of butter and confectioners' sugar in this sweetened dough, it is very malleable and easy to work with. The baking powder also gives the crust a nice lift. If you don't need all the dough, freeze any that you don't use.

2 cups unbleached all-purpose flour

½ cup confectioners' sugar

2 teaspoons baking powder

½ teaspoon salt

1½ sticks (6 ounces) cold unsalted butter, cut into small cubes

2 egg yolks

2 tablespoons cold milk

1. Place the flour, confectioners' sugar, baking powder, and salt in a food processor and pulse briefly to mix. Add the butter and pulse until it is cut in and the mixture resembles coarse meal. Add the egg yolks and milk and process just until the dough is smooth and evenly moistened. Do not process until the dough forms a ball, or it will be tough.

2. Remove the dough from the processor, divide it in half, and press each half into a ball. Flatten into two disks, wrap well, and refrigerate for at least 30 minutes before using.

Baking Tip: If you prefer to make your dough by hand, simply combine the dry ingredients in a mixing bowl, cut in the butter, and then stir in the beaten egg yolks and milk.

LATTICE DOUGH

MAKES ENOUGH DOUGH FOR 1 LATTICE TOP

This dough is very forgiving; it can be rolled out several times without becoming stiff and dry. Because it's so flexible, it's ideal for making lattice strips (see technique on page 11).

1 cup unbleached all-purpose flour

6 tablespoons confectioners' sugar

6 tablespoons cold unsalted butter, cut into small cubes

1 egg yolk

1   Place the flour and confectioners' sugar in a food processor and whirl briefly to blend. Scatter the butter evenly over the top of the dry ingredients. Pulse to cut in the butter, processing until no lumps are visible and the mixture is the texture of cornmeal.

2   Add the egg yolk and pulse to blend, mixing only until the dough comes together; do not overprocess.

Country Cakes

Double-Chocolate Fudge Cake (page 61) with Chocolate Glaze (page 62)

Cakes will forever vie for our attention as the supreme dessert, and as cake lovers like to point out, "Nobody ever asks for a birthday pie."

We take our cakes seriously in the South. They're a versatile dessert that can suit just about any hankering or occasion, form or flavor. Indeed, many of the Loveless cakes seem to have personalities of their own; some even bear names that reveal their origins. Our cakes range from the most modest angel food cake to a decadent coconut cake filled with coconut milk, coconut flakes, *and* rich cream. There's Big Momma's Blackberry Jam Cake, rising in three layers from the plate just like the towering Harpeth Valley Hummingbird Cake with layers of cream cheese frosting.

Southern bakers know how to put the full pantry to use, employing some surprising ingredients. Coca-Cola cakes have long been a favorite in the South, but have you tried our Root Beer Float Cake? Or Guess Again Tomato Cake with Pecans and Raisins? Bet your guests won't figure out that the slice in front of them, laden with nuts and fruit, also has tomato juice—they'll

just marvel at the moist, unique flavor. Our Chocolate Mashed Potato Cake has its own surprise. The ingredients call for last night's leftover mashed potatoes baked right into the buttermilk batter. You'll have fun explaining that one to your guests, if you choose to.

The whole cakes and generous slices we keep in the display case at the Loveless beckon customers as soon as they walk into the cafe. When our regulars spy a piece of one of their favorites, you can expect them to tap on the glass and give the hostess a little nod, ensuring that they will not be disappointed when the dinner dishes are cleared. You see, our seasoned customers know they'd better make sure that their piece of cake accompanies them to the table, before the meal.

BIG MOMMA'S BLACKBERRY JAM CAKE

MAKES A 9-INCH TRIPLE-LAYER CAKE; SERVES 12 TO 16

Here's a real Southern recipe from Mark Curtis, one of the Loveless staff, adapted for our dessert menu. The cake was made by his grandmother, who, believe it or not and with all due respect to Tennessee Williams, really was called "Big Momma." Contrary to what you might expect, the jam is not used as a filling but goes right into the buttermilk batter.

1 cup golden raisins

1 cup walnut halves or pieces

3 cups cake flour

1 teaspoon ground cinnamon

1 teaspoon ground allspice

1 teaspoon freshly grated nutmeg

½ teaspoon ground cloves

1 teaspoon baking soda

2 sticks (8 ounces) unsalted butter, softened

1½ cups packed dark brown sugar

½ teaspoon salt

3 eggs

1 cup blackberry jam, preferably seedless

1 cup buttermilk

Coconut Caramel Glaze (page 60)

1. Preheat the oven to 350°F. Grease three 9-inch cake pans. Line the bottoms with parchment paper and grease the paper.

2. Put the golden raisins in a small saucepan. Add water to cover and bring to a boil. Remove from the heat and let cool completely; drain well. Meanwhile, spread out the walnuts in a small baking pan and toast in the oven for 5 to 7 minutes, until lightly browned and fragrant. Let cool, then chop evenly.

3. Sift the flour, cinnamon, allspice, nutmeg, cloves, and baking soda into a bowl and set aside. With an electric mixer, cream the butter with the brown sugar and salt in a large bowl at medium-low speed until light and fluffy. Add the eggs, one at a time, scraping the bowl once. Add the jam and mix it in completely. Add the reserved dry ingredients alternately with the buttermilk, scraping the bowl once or twice. Fold in the raisins and walnuts. Divide the batter among the pans.

4. Bake for 28 to 32 minutes, or until a toothpick or cake tester inserted in the center comes out clean. Let the cakes cool in the pans for 10 minutes, then invert them onto a rack, remove the paper, and let cool completely.

5. To assemble the cake, place one layer bottom side up on a cake stand or dessert platter. Spoon one-third of the glaze over the cake, leaving a ½-inch border around the edge. Top with the next layer and repeat with more glaze. Set the last layer on top and pour the remaining glaze onto the cake. Spread just to the edge, letting the glaze drizzle down the sides. Let set for about 1 hour before cutting.

Coconut Caramel Glaze

2 cups packed dark brown sugar

2 sticks (8 ounces) unsalted butter, softened

1 cup half-and-half

1 cup sweetened shredded coconut

¼ cup unbleached all-purpose flour

1 teaspoon vanilla extract

1 Place the brown sugar, butter, half-and-half, coconut, and flour in a large shallow, heavy saucepan. Set over medium-low heat and cook, stirring, until the mixture is completely blended and just begins to boil.

2 Continue to boil gently, whisking occasionally, until the glaze thickens slightly, 7 to 10 minutes. Remove from the heat, stir in the vanilla, and pour the glaze into a bowl. Let cool slightly. Press a sheet of plastic wrap directly onto the surface to prevent a skin from forming and refrigerate until tepid and thickened but still runny enough to drop from a spoon like a thick sauce, about 1 hour.

Baking Tip: If the glaze hardens, warm it gently in a microwave on the lowest setting until it becomes just thin enough to spread.

To make our Loveless jams, we go through 600 pounds each of blackberries, strawberries, and peaches every week.

DOUBLE-CHOCOLATE FUDGE CAKE

MAKES A 9-INCH TRIPLE-LAYER CAKE; SERVES 14 TO 16

What's a pound of chocolate or so among friends? At the Loveless, we can go through one of these tall beauties in an hour without blinking. Because it's chocolate and it's three layers high, it makes a great birthday cake for chocolate lovers. And since it is drip-glazed rather than frosted, you don't need to be a pastry chef to make it look fantastic.

2⅔ cups unbleached all-purpose flour

2 cups sugar

⅓ cup unsweetened cocoa powder

2¼ teaspoons baking soda

½ teaspoon ground cinnamon

¾ teaspoon salt

1½ sticks (6 ounces) unsalted butter, softened

1⅓ cups sour cream

3 ounces unsweetened chocolate, melted and slightly cooled (see page 36)

3 eggs

1½ teaspoons vanilla extract

Chocolate Glaze (page 62)

1 Preheat the oven to 350°F. Grease three 9-inch cake pans. Line the bottoms with parchment paper and grease the paper.

2 Place the flour, sugar, cocoa powder, baking soda, cinnamon, and salt in a large mixing bowl and blend on low speed for about 30 seconds to mix. Add the butter, sour cream, and unsweetened chocolate. Continue to beat on low until thoroughly combined. Scrape the bowl and raise the speed to medium; mix until light and fluffy, about 3 minutes. Add the eggs, one at a time. Add the vanilla and mix to blend well. Divide the batter evenly among the pans.

3 Bake until a toothpick or cake tester inserted in the center comes out clean, about 30 minutes. Let the cakes cool in the pans for 5 to 10 minutes, then turn them out onto a rack and let cool completely.

4 To decorate the cake, place one layer bottom side up on a cake stand or dessert platter. Top with ⅔ cup of the Chocolate Glaze, spreading it to the edge of the cake. Set another layer on top and repeat. Set the top layer in place and pour the remaining glaze slowly over the center. Using a spatula, guide the glaze to the edges of the cake as you turn the stand so that the chocolate slowly spills over the sides and drips down the cake.

Photograph on page 55.

Chocolate Glaze

MAKES ABOUT 3 CUPS

1 pound bittersweet or
semisweet chocolate, chopped

1 cup half-and-half

Place the bittersweet chocolate and half-and-half in a microwave-safe bowl and heat on the lowest setting or the defrost setting for 1 minute; stir well. Microwave for 30 seconds and stir again. Repeat, if necessary, until the mixture is completely melted and smooth. Let cool until tepid; do not refrigerate.

SOUTHERN-STYLE COCONUT CAKE

MAKES A DOUBLE-LAYER 9-INCH CAKE; SERVES 12

At the cafe, we usually serve this cake with a cream cheese frosting, but the classic Southern presentation is with a billowy white meringue like the one found here. Either way, it's one of the stars of our dessert showcase, which tempts everyone on the way in and causes many to linger for an extra bite on the way out.

4 egg whites

⅓ cup milk

1½ teaspoons vanilla extract

2⅓ cups self-rising flour

1¾ cups sugar

1½ sticks (6 ounces) unsalted butter, softened

¾ cup canned unsweetened coconut milk

Seven-Minute Meringue Frosting (page 64)

2½ cups sweetened shredded coconut

Baking Tip: Self-rising flour is a Southern staple, since it's what we almost always use in biscuits. If you don't have any on hand, you can substitute 2⅓ cups cake flour and 3½ teaspoons baking powder.

1 Preheat the oven to 350°F. Grease two 9-inch cake pans. Line the bottoms with parchment paper and grease the paper.

2 In a small bowl, whisk the egg whites, milk, and vanilla together just until blended. Place the flour and sugar in a large bowl and blend with a mixer on low speed for 30 seconds to combine. Add the butter and coconut milk and mix to combine. Scrape the bowl, raise the speed to medium, and beat until light and fluffy, 2 to 3 minutes. Add the egg white mixture in two or three additions, scraping the bowl and blending thoroughly. Divide the batter between the pans.

3 Bake for 35 to 40 minutes, or until a toothpick or cake tester inserted in the center comes out clean. Let the cake cool in the pans for 10 minutes. Turn the layers out onto a wire rack and cool completely before frosting.

4 To decorate the cake, place one layer, bottom side up, on a cake stand or dessert platter. Top with 1 cup of the frosting, spreading it evenly to the edges. Sprinkle ½ cup coconut over the frosting and top with the second layer. Spread the remaining frosting over the top and sides of the cake. Cover the cake completely with the remaining 2 cups coconut by sprinkling it on top and pressing it lightly onto the sides.

Photograph on page 65.

Seven-Minute Meringue Frosting

4 egg whites

¼ teaspoon cream of tartar

1¼ cups sugar

3 tablespoons light corn syrup

1 teaspoon vanilla extract

Baking Tip: If you prefer a frosting that is less sweet than meringue and will hold up longer, follow the recipe for Cream Cheese Frosting on page 70, using these measurements: 8 ounces cream cheese, 1 stick unsalted butter, 4 cups confectioners' sugar, and 2 teaspoons vanilla extract.

1. Place the egg whites and cream of tartar in the bowl of an electric mixer and beat lightly to blend. Set aside.

2. In a small saucepan, combine the sugar, corn syrup, and 2 tablespoons water. Stir with a spoon to mix. If any sugar clings to the side of the pan, use a wet pastry brush to wash it down. Set the pan over medium-low heat, cover, and slowly bring to a boil. (You'll have to peek to see when it reaches a boil, but do not stir.) Allow the syrup to boil for 1 minute, covered. Remove the lid and insert a candy thermometer. Continue to cook until the syrup reaches 238°F, which will happen pretty quickly.

3. Turn the electric mixer to medium-low speed and slowly pour the sugar syrup into the egg whites as you whip them, trying to avoid hitting the beaters, which might splatter. Continue to whip until the egg whites are almost stiff but droop slightly at the peak when the beater is lifted. Beat in the vanilla until well mixed. Use at once.

CHOCOLATE MASHED POTATO CAKE

MAKES A 9 BY 12-INCH SHEET CAKE; SERVES 12 TO 16

We often have leftover mashed potatoes at the cafe, which we're happy to put to good use. They add moisture and structure to many breads and cakes, such as this one. Because you cannot taste the potato in the finished product, no one will know it's there. This is a stiff batter that is best prepared in a stand mixer or with a very strong hand mixer.

2 cups sugar

1¾ cups cake flour

1½ teaspoons baking soda

¾ cup warm (not hot), unseasoned mashed potatoes

4 ounces unsweetened chocolate, melted and slightly cooled (see page 36)

1 stick (4 ounces) unsalted butter, softened

2 eggs

¾ cup buttermilk

1 teaspoon vanilla extract

Light Chocolate Frosting (recipe follows)

1. Preheat the oven to 350°F. Grease a 9 by 12-inch rectangular baking dish.

2. Place the sugar, cake flour, and baking soda in a mixing bowl and beat on low speed to combine, about 1 minute. Add the mashed potatoes, melted chocolate, and butter; mix until blended. Raise the speed to medium and beat until fluffy, about 2 minutes.

3. In another bowl, whisk the eggs, buttermilk, and vanilla together until blended. Pour into the chocolate mixture in two additions, scraping the bowl well between additions. Turn the batter into the greased baking dish.

4. Bake for 45 to 50 minutes, or until a toothpick or cake tester inserted in the center comes out clean. Let the cake cool completely in the dish before frosting the top with Light Chocolate Frosting. Cut into squares to serve.

Light Chocolate Frosting

6 tablespoons unsalted butter, softened

1½ cups confectioners' sugar, sifted

1½ ounces unsweetened chocolate, melted and slightly cooled (see page 36)

2 tablespoons half-and-half

1. Place the butter in a mixing bowl. Add the confectioners' sugar and blend on low speed to combine. Raise the speed to medium and beat until fluffy, about 2 minutes.

2. Add the chocolate and mix well, scraping the bowl to incorporate completely. Add the half-and-half and beat until blended. Use immediately.

HARPETH VALLEY HUMMINGBIRD CAKE

MAKES A 9-INCH TRIPLE-LAYER CAKE; SERVES 16

Before we became the Loveless Cafe and Motel, the original name was the Harpeth Valley Tea Room, after the name of this area, which is situated close to the Harpeth River. This is a Southern classic: a rich, moist cinnamon cake studded with banana, pineapple, and pecan pieces and slathered with cream cheese frosting. Whether or not the Harpeth Valley Tea Room actually served this particular cake is lost in history, but it is definitely a favorite among the staff and customers of today's Loveless Cafe, and this book would be incomplete without it.

2 cups pecan pieces

3 medium bananas, cut into chunks

1½ cups fresh pineapple chunks (about ½ pound)

2 cups packed light brown sugar

1 cup canola or other neutral vegetable oil

3 eggs

1½ teaspoons vanilla extract

3½ cups unbleached all-purpose flour

1¼ teaspoons baking soda

1¼ teaspoons ground cinnamon

1 teaspoon salt

Cream Cheese Frosting (page 70)

1. Preheat the oven to 350°F. Grease three 9-inch cake pans. Line the bottoms with parchment paper and grease the paper.

2. Place the pecans on a baking sheet and toast in the oven for 5 to 7 minutes. Let cool completely. Measure out 1 cup for the cake and reserve the rest for the garnish.

3. In a food processor, combine the banana and pineapple chunks. Pulse until the fruit is chopped to the size of peas. Pour into a mixing bowl. Add the toasted pecans, brown sugar, oil, eggs, and vanilla. Whisk by hand until blended. Sift the flour, baking soda, cinnamon, and salt over the fruit mixture. With a spatula, fold the batter until evenly blended. Divide among the pans.

4. Bake for 30 to 35 minutes, until a toothpick or cake tester inserted in the center comes out clean. Let the cakes cool in the pans for 10 to 15 minutes, then turn them out onto racks, peel off the paper, and let them cool completely.

5. To decorate the cake, place one layer bottom side up on a cake stand or dessert platter. Top with ¾ cup frosting and spread evenly to the edge of the cake. Repeat with a second layer and another ¾ cup frosting. Add the top layer and spread the remaining frosting over the top and sides of the cake. Use a spoon or spatula to make a swirl pattern in the frosting. Decorate the sides of the cake with the reserved pecans.

Cream Cheese Frosting

MAKES ABOUT 4 CUPS

10 ounces cream cheese, softened

1 stick (4 ounces) plus 2 tablespoons unsalted butter, softened

5 cups confectioners' sugar

2 teaspoons vanilla extract

Place the cream cheese and butter in a mixing bowl and beat with an electric mixer on medium speed until completely blended. Sift the confectioners' sugar onto the mixture in several additions, beating thoroughly in between. Add the vanilla and beat until the frosting is light and fluffy but still holds its shape, 3 to 5 minutes. Use immediately.

Baking Tip: Do not use reduced-fat or nonfat cream cheese. The consistency will not be the same.

Celebrity Row

Lots of country musicians pass through the Loveless. Either they live around Nashville, they're here to produce a record, or they're on tour. We serve up comfort food, and the cafe feels like home to many who spend weeks, if not months, out on the road. At the Loveless they get a chance to relax over a meal like their mama might have made. The official restaurant policy is to respect their privacy and treat them just like our other customers who are not celebrities.

That's all well and good, but every now and then our policy backfires. Kenny Chesney came in one Sunday and was told summarily that there was a two-hour wait for a table. So he left. Needless to say, there was something of an uproar when the powers that be heard we actually had turned away a star; privacy is one thing, but accommodations can be made. The staff felt terrible they'd lost the chance to serve such a big talent. (Just for the record, Kenny did come back a week or so later.)

Faith Hill comes in with her husband and kids. Sometimes she's dressed up like the star she is, but she also comes in dressed casually, with no makeup at all, her hair tucked under a baseball cap, looking just like anyone else's unassuming mom.

Posh or laid-back, celebrity or common folk, at the Loveless we welcome all our customers like members of the family.

ROOT BEER FLOAT CAKE

MAKES A 10-INCH BUNDT CAKE; SERVES 12 TO 16

Cooking with soda pop is an old Southern tradition. Hams are often braised in cola, and local cookbooks are filled with recipes for Dr Pepper cakes, 7UP cakes, cola cakes, and more. Our Loveless beauty is inspired by the beverage that was so popular in the 1950s, when the cafe and motel were first established. Topped off with a creamy white glaze, this popular dessert tastes like a root beer float on a plate.

2 cups root beer, preferably naturally flavored, such as Natural Brew

3¼ cups cake flour

2 tablespoons unsweetened cocoa powder (*not* Dutch process)

1½ teaspoons baking soda

½ teaspoon ground cloves

1½ sticks (6 ounces) unsalted butter, softened

1½ cups packed dark brown sugar

2 teaspoons vanilla extract

1 teaspoon salt

2 eggs

Vanilla Glaze (recipe follows)

1 Preheat the oven to 350°F. Grease and flour a 10-cup Bundt pan. Open the root beer and let it stand while you begin the batter to let some of the effervescence subside.

2 Sift the cake flour, cocoa powder, baking soda, and cloves into a bowl and set aside. In a large mixing bowl, cream the butter with the brown sugar, vanilla, and salt on medium-low speed until light and fluffy. Add the eggs, one at a time, and scrape down the bowl. Add the dry ingredients alternately with the root beer, beating on low speed and scraping the bowl well between additions. Pour the batter into the prepared pan.

3 Bake for 55 minutes, or until a toothpick or cake tester inserted in the center comes out clean. Let the cake cool in the pan for about 15 minutes, then unmold and let cool on a rack. Drizzle the glaze over the cake, spreading it lightly so that the entire surface is coated.

Vanilla Glaze

MAKES ABOUT ¾ CUP

2 cups confectioners' sugar

2 tablespoons unsalted butter, melted

⅓ cup milk

1 teaspoon vanilla extract

Sift the confectioners' sugar into a bowl. Add the melted butter, milk, and vanilla. Whisk until smooth and creamy. Use at once.

PEACH UPSIDE-DOWN CAKE

MAKES A 10-INCH SINGLE-LAYER CAKE; SERVES 8

Upside-down cakes are popular in the South, especially because we have such fine local fruit to work with. Peach preserves are one of the best-selling items in the Loveless gift shop, so it's no surprise the flavor is popular on top of cake. Upside-down cakes should be served as soon as possible after baking, while they are still warm, with the buttery caramel that forms during baking drizzling down the sides of the rich, tender cake.

1 pound ripe peaches

4 tablespoons unsalted butter

¼ cup light honey, such as wildflower

¼ teaspoon ground cinnamon

1¼ cups sugar

1 cup heavy cream

1 teaspoon vanilla extract

2 eggs

1¾ cups self-rising flour

½ teaspoon salt

1 Preheat the oven to 350°F. Drop the peaches into a saucepan of boiling water for 15 to 30 seconds. Remove with a skimmer and rinse under cold running water. Rub off the skins and slice the peaches about ¼ inch thick. There should be about 3 cups.

2 Place a 10-inch cast-iron skillet over medium heat. Add the butter, honey, cinnamon, and ¼ cup of the sugar. Stir as the butter and sugar melt. Continue cooking, stirring occasionally, until the syrup boils and thickens slightly, 2 to 3 minutes. Remove from the heat. Carefully arrange the peach slices on top of the warm caramel in a decorative pattern, working from the outer edge to the center; set aside.

3 To make the batter, place the cream and vanilla in a mixing bowl and whip on medium-high speed until soft peaks form. Gradually beat in the remaining 1 cup sugar in a steady stream and continue mixing until soft; do not overmix. Add the eggs and beat until soft peaks form again. Sift the flour and salt over the top of the batter and fold in until evenly mixed. Gently pour the batter over the peaches in the skillet, spreading it evenly.

4 Place the skillet in the oven with a baking sheet placed on the shelf below to catch any drips. Bake for about 40 minutes, until a toothpick or cake tester inserted in the center comes out clean. Let the cake stand for 5 to 10 minutes. Place a heatproof serving dish on top and carefully invert so that the cake drops straight down over the center of the dish. To serve, use a serrated knife to cut through the peaches and cake.

PINEAPPLE UPSIDE-DOWN CAKE

MAKES A 10-INCH SINGLE-LAYER CAKE; SERVES 8

Using fresh rather than canned pineapple gives this classic a much more intense flavor. This has such a light crumb that it makes a nice breakfast cake.

1 fully ripened fresh pineapple

1½ sticks (6 ounces) unsalted butter, softened

¼ cup packed light brown sugar

¼ cup light honey, such as wildflower

1⅓ cups granulated sugar

1 teaspoon vanilla extract

¼ teaspoon salt

2 eggs

2⅓ cups cake flour

2 teaspoons baking powder

⅓ cup milk

Baking Tip: If you do not want to bother with cleaning a fresh pineapple, look for one that is already trimmed, cored, and sliced at the supermarket. The flavor will still be much better than anything in a can.

1. Preheat the oven to 350°F. With a sharp knife, trim off the bottom of the pineapple. Holding it upright by the stem, cut down all around to remove the rind; then cut off the top. Split the pineapple in half lengthwise. Cut out the fibrous central core by making a long V-shaped notch, slicing down at an angle on either side of the center. Cut the cored pineapple into slices no thicker than ¼ inch; cut these pieces in half to make triangular slices. Chop enough of the less perfect slices to yield ¼ cup chopped pineapple; set the chopped pineapple aside for the batter.

2. Place a 10-inch cast-iron skillet over medium heat. Place ½ stick of the butter, the brown sugar, and the honey in the pan. Stir as the butter and sugar melt. When the mixture begins to boil gently, continue to cook, stirring, for about 2 minutes, until the caramel thickens slightly. Remove from the heat.

3. Carefully arrange the pineapple slices on the warm caramel, starting at the outer edge and working in toward the center. Slightly overlap the slices to prevent large gaps in the design. Set the skillet aside while you prepare the batter.

4. In a large mixing bowl, cream the remaining stick of butter with the granulated sugar, vanilla, and salt until light and fluffy. Add the eggs one at a time, beating well and scraping the sides of the bowl after each addition. Sift the flour and baking powder over the batter. Fold a few times, then add the milk and fold together until blended. Finally, fold in the chopped pineapple with any juice that has accumulated. Gently dollop the batter over the pineapple in the skillet to cover the fruit without dislodging the design.

5 Place an empty baking pan on the lower rack in the oven to catch any drips. Bake in the center of the oven for about 50 minutes, until a toothpick or cake tester inserted in the center comes out clean. Let the cake stand for 5 to 10 minutes. Place a heatproof serving dish on top and carefully invert the two so that the cake drops straight down over the center of the serving dish. To serve, use a serrated knife to cut through the pineapple and cake.

RED VELVET CAKE

MAKES AN 8-INCH DOUBLE-LAYER CAKE; SERVES 8 TO 10

A slice of red velvet cake looks just as its name implies—soft and red—though its flavor base is cocoa. A big hit on Valentine's Day, the dessert is popular for the holidays as well. One VIP customer has us bake dozens to give as gifts for Christmas. Rich with butter and eggs and cloaked in an ivory cream cheese and butter vanilla frosting, this is a cake that holds up well for at least three days.

2½ cups cake flour

⅓ cup unsweetened cocoa powder (*not* Dutch process)

1 teaspoon baking soda

2 tablespoons liquid red food color

1 cup buttermilk

2½ sticks (10 ounces) unsalted butter, softened

2 cups packed dark brown sugar

1 teaspoon vanilla extract

½ teaspoon salt

2 whole eggs plus 2 egg yolks

1 tablespoon distilled white or cider vinegar

Cream Cheese Frosting (page 70), made with the proportions in step 5

1. Preheat the oven to 350°F. Grease two 8-inch cake pans. Line the bottoms with parchment paper and grease the paper.

2. Sift the flour, cocoa, and baking soda into a bowl and whisk briefly to combine; set aside. Stir the red food color into the buttermilk and set aside.

3. In a large mixing bowl, cream the butter with the brown sugar, vanilla, and salt on medium-low speed until light and fluffy, 3 to 5 minutes. Add the eggs and egg yolks slowly, beating and scraping the bowl to ensure that they are completely incorporated. On low speed, add the dry ingredients alternately with the colored buttermilk. To prevent streaking in the cake, be sure to scrape the sides of the bowl well as you mix the batter. Finally, stir in the vinegar by hand. Divide the batter between the cake pans.

4. Bake for 35 to 40 minutes, or until a toothpick or cake tester inserted in the center comes out clean. Let the layers cool in the pans for 10 minutes. Then turn them out onto a wire rack, peel off the paper, and let cool completely.

5. Make the frosting using 8 ounces cream cheese, 1 stick unsalted butter, 4 cups confectioners' sugar, and 2 teaspoons vanilla extract.

6. To decorate the cake, place one layer bottom side up on a cake plate. Spread ¾ cup of the cream cheese frosting evenly over the cake right to the edges. Add the second layer and use the remaining frosting to decorate the sides and top by gently swirling it over the cake.

GUESS AGAIN TOMATO CAKE WITH PECANS AND RAISINS

MAKES AN 8-INCH TUBE CAKE; SERVES 8

Not one of our waitstaff could guess the source of the unique flavor in this moist dessert. Inspired by the old-fashioned back-of-the-can tomato soup cake, this one uses tomato juice rather than soup, which imparts a bit of color and a taste you just can't put your finger on. We like having fun at the Loveless. Many days, crossword puzzles and guessing games circulate through the dining room, and a recipe with a secret ingredient has special appeal for many of our customers.

½ cup golden raisins

½ cup pecan pieces

2 cups cake flour

¾ teaspoon baking soda

1 teaspoon ground cinnamon

½ teaspoon ground allspice

¼ teaspoon ground cloves

¼ teaspoon freshly grated nutmeg

1 stick (4 ounces) plus 2 tablespoons unsalted butter, softened

1¼ cups packed dark brown sugar

1 teaspoon vanilla extract

1 egg

1 cup tomato juice

Vanilla Glaze (page 71)

1. Preheat the oven to 350°F. Grease and flour a 6- to 8-cup tube pan. Place the golden raisins in a small saucepan, cover with water, and bring to a boil. Remove from the heat and let the raisins plump in the water until they cool; drain well.

2. Meanwhile, toast the pecans on a baking sheet in the oven for 5 to 7 minutes, until lightly colored and fragrant. Transfer to a dish and let cool.

3. In a mixing bowl, combine the cake flour, baking soda, cinnamon, allspice, cloves, and nutmeg. Set the dry ingredients aside.

4. In a large mixing bowl, beat the butter on medium-low speed for 1 minute. Add the brown sugar and vanilla and beat until light and fluffy, 2 to 3 minutes. Add the egg and mix completely, scraping the bowl once. Sift one-third of the dry ingredients over the butter mixture, fold a few times by hand with a rubber spatula, and add half of the tomato juice. Fold a few times; sift half of the remaining spiced flour over the batter, add the remaining juice, and fold a few times. Add the remaining flour, and fold the batter gently until no streaks remain. Add the raisins and pecans. Fold gently to incorporate evenly. Pour the batter into the prepared pan.

Hints for Easy Baking

Some people are intimidated by baking a cake from scratch. But with these no-fail recipes, preparing the pans is probably the hardest part of the process. Here are a few tips to guarantee success:

• Measure flour using the scoop-and-sweep method: Dip the measuring cup into the container of flour without packing it down and level off the top with the straight back of a knife or the edge of a long spatula.

• Either large or extra-large eggs will work for these recipes.

• Notice that when an electric mixer is used, the speed is low or medium-low. Contrary to expectations, gentler whipping actually incorporates more air, which results in a higher, lighter cake.

• Check your baking temperature with an oven thermometer every six months and adjust as necessary.

5 Bake for 45 minutes, or until a toothpick or cake tester inserted in the thickest part of the cake comes out clean. Let cool in the pan for 10 minutes, then unmold and cool completely on a wire rack. Using a large spoon, ladle the glaze over the top of the cake, completely covering the top and letting the excess drip down the sides randomly.

Photograph on page 83.

SORGHUM SPICE CAKE WITH LEMON GLAZE

MAKES A 10-INCH BUNDT CAKE; SERVES 12 TO 16

Sorghum is something you don't find easily once you leave the South. Traditionally served with hot biscuits or corn bread, it is good for many things. Similar to molasses but much milder, the syrup adds a rich flavor and a darker color to baked goods. At the cafe we offer sorghum made by an Amish community in Kentucky with our biscuits, and in the dessert kitchen we use it in everything from cookies to cakes. In this cake, sorghum allows the spices to shine through, while the mildly tart lemon glaze adds a touch of brightness.

1 cup packed dark brown sugar

1 cup canola or other neutral vegetable oil

1 cup sorghum

3 eggs

½ cup buttermilk

3 cups unbleached all-purpose flour

2 teaspoons baking soda

½ teaspoon salt

1 tablespoon plus 1 teaspoon ground ginger

2¼ teaspoons ground cinnamon

¾ teaspoon ground cardamom

¾ teaspoon ground cloves

¾ teaspoon freshly grated nutmeg

Fresh Lemon Glaze
(recipe follows)

1. Preheat the oven to 350°F. Grease a 10-inch Bundt pan or plain tube pan.

2. In a large mixing bowl, break up any large lumps in the brown sugar with your fingertipss. Whisk in the oil, sorghum, eggs, and buttermilk.

3. Sift the flour, baking soda, salt, ginger, cinnamon, cardamom, cloves, and nutmeg onto the egg mixture. Using a rubber spatula, fold until the batter is evenly mixed. Scrape into the prepared pan.

4. Bake in the center of the oven for 50 to 55 minutes, until a toothpick or cake tester inserted in the center comes out clean. Let the cake stand in the pan for 10 minutes, then unmold onto a wire rack to cool completely. Pour the glaze over the cake, allowing it to drizzle down the sides. Let set before slicing.

Fresh Lemon Glaze

MAKES ABOUT 1 CUP

3 cups confectioners' sugar

¼ cup plus 2 tablespoons freshly squeezed lemon juice

1 teaspoon grated lemon zest

Sift the confectioners' sugar into a bowl. Whisk in the lemon juice and zest. Use at once.

The Loveless kitchen goes through 6,000 eggs each week. That's 500 dozen!

CARAMEL APPLE CAKE

MAKES AN 8-INCH BUNDT CAKE; SERVES 8

Tennessee has innumerable county fairs that vie for attention all through the summer and early fall. The Wilson County Fair in Lebanon, just east of Nashville, attracts half a million visitors every August. Amid all the typical fried foods, sausages, and kettle corn are gorgeous caramel-coated apples on a stick, and that's what inspired us to put this luscious apple cake coated in caramel on the menu.

½ cup pecan pieces

2 eggs

1½ cups packed dark brown sugar

1 cup canola or other neutral vegetable oil

2 Granny Smith apples, peeled, cored, and cut into ¼-inch dice

2 cups unbleached all-purpose flour

1½ teaspoons ground cinnamon

1 teaspoon freshly grated nutmeg

½ teaspoon ground cardamom

¾ teaspoon baking soda

1 cup Drunken Caramel Sauce (page 206)

Baking Tip: If you don't want to make your own caramel sauce, you can buy it, but be sure it is a thick sauce, such as an ice cream topping. Mexican *cajeta* (see Sources, page 210) or *leche quemada* works quite well too.

1 Preheat the oven to 350°F. Grease and flour a 6- to 8-cup Bundt pan.

2 Place the pecans in a small baking pan and toast them in the oven for 5 to 7 minutes, until lightly colored and fragrant. Let cool.

3 Place the eggs, brown sugar, and oil in a large bowl and whisk until smooth. Add the pecans and apples and stir with a spatula to combine. Sift the flour, cinnamon, nutmeg, cardamom, and baking soda over the mixture. Fold together until combined so that no streaks of flour remain. Scrape the batter into the prepared pan.

4 Bake for 1 hour 10 minutes, or until a toothpick or cake tester inserted in the center comes out clean. Let the cake cool in the pan for about 20 minutes, then turn it out onto a rack and place the rack over a baking sheet. Using a fork, poke holes all around the sides and top of the cake.

5 If the caramel sauce is not in a liquid state, heat it gently on the lowest setting in the microwave until it pours like honey. Drizzle the caramel slowly over the cake in an effort to cover the entire cake with a thin layer of glaze. If the caramel pools on the pan below, scoop it up and drizzle it over the cake again; the more you get on the cake, the better. Allow the caramel to set and the cake to cool completely before slicing.

Caramel Apple Cake (top), Guess Again Tomato Cake with Pecans and Raisins (middle, page 78), and Spiced Pumpkin–Chocolate Chip Tea Cake (bottom, page 147)

PASTEL ANGEL FOOD CAKE

MAKES AN 8-INCH TUBE CAKE; SERVES 6 TO 8

Perhaps because they are so tall and light, angel food cakes are very popular in the South. At our supermarkets in Nashville, they're sold frosted and airbrushed bright shades of pink, blue, and green. Since we serve all-natural products in the desserts at the cafe, we set about to create an angel food cake colored with only natural ingredients. As it happens, blackberry turns out a lovely shade of lavender and tart cherry a winsome pale pink.

Because it is fat free, angel food cake gets sticky pretty fast, especially in the humid South, so it's best served the same day it's baked. It also works well as a base for fruit shortcake.

¾ cup unsweetened blackberry juice or tart cherry juice

¾ cup cake flour

⅔ cup confectioners' sugar

¼ teaspoon salt

1 cup egg whites (6 to 8)

½ teaspoon cream of tartar

⅔ cup granulated sugar

1 teaspoon vanilla extract

1 Pour the fruit juice into a small nonreactive saucepan and boil gently over medium-low heat until reduced to ¼ cup, about 10 minutes. Remove from the heat and let cool completely.

2 Preheat the oven to 350°F. Sift the flour, confectioners' sugar, and salt together and set aside.

3 Place the egg whites in a large mixing bowl with the cream of tartar and whip until foamy. Gradually beat in the granulated sugar; continue to whip until the peaks are stiff but not dry and the tips droop slightly when the beaters are lifted.

4 Fold in the vanilla and concentrated fruit juice by hand. Sift one-third of the flour mixture over the whites and fold in very gently. Repeat with half of the remaining flour, then fold in the rest just until evenly blended. Scrape the batter into an ungreased 6-cup tube pan. Run a blunt knife around the batter at the edges of the pan to remove any air pockets.

Baking Tips

- The key to success with this cake is to measure the egg whites by the cup. Egg sizes can vary greatly, and the cup measure guarantees that you will have the exact proportion necessary for a tender cake.

- Angel food is a type of sponge cake, which means you should not use a nonstick pan, and the tube pan should *not* be greased. A dry side allows the cake to attach itself to the pan and rise properly.

5 Bake for 35 to 40 minutes, until a toothpick or cake tester inserted in the center comes out clean. Remove the pan from the oven and invert it onto a rack. Let cool in this position until the pan and cake are cooled completely to room temperature, about 1 hour.

6 To remove the cake from the pan, run a bamboo skewer around the edges of the cake, invert the pan onto a cake plate, and gently tap the cake out. Use a serrated knife to cut into 1½- to 2-inch-thick slices. Serve within a couple hours if possible.

The Loveless sits on the side of Highway 100 in the little community of Pasquo, just outside of Nashville. Motel operations ceased in 1985, and the units were converted into the Hams & Jams Country Market and other locally owned shops.

Crisps, Cobblers, and Shortcakes

Angel Berry-Rhubarb Shortcake (page 113)

Southerners like to claim cobbler

as an American invention, but it most likely originated in nineteenth-century Europe. No matter where cobbler started, Southern cooks surely elevated the dessert. Overwhelmed with basketfuls of season-ripe fruit, and knowing they would have to face throngs of family and friends for untold summer socials, these industrious cooks ignored form and formality and went straight for function and flavor.

At the Loveless, cobblers, crisps, and their entire family of more casual desserts showcase a full array of fruit. Nothing stands in the way of their fragrant, concentrated filling but a cloaking of crust as varied as the regional names of these desserts. You don't need an expert to trace the roots of slumps and buckles, grunts and crisps—a quick glance at their uneven tops usually offers a pretty good explanation. However, while the name *pandowdy* might sound dull, give our Raspberry Plum Pandowdy a try. The excitement is all in the taste.

These desserts, along with shortcakes, provide the perfect marriage of pastry and fruit. They make great partners when bushes are brimming with berries, and work equally well in winter when frozen fruits can help brighten the longest of nights. Cobblers and shortcakes also take kindly to scoops of ice cream, homemade whipped toppings, and any variety of flavored creams. At the Loveless, we like to add citrus notes to lift the fruit flavors, and for a newfangled baking trick, our Blackberry Cobbler with Cinnamon-Swirl Biscuits is made all the more fragrant thanks to the light perfume of rose water.

The homey sensibility of cobblers, crisps, and shortcakes makes comfort palpable; it's what the Loveless Cafe is all about, a kind of Southern culinary sanctuary on earth.

APPLE CRISP
WITH WALNUT-OAT STREUSEL TOPPING

SERVES 4

Even in a casual restaurant like the Loveless, if you're going to serve a dessert this simple, you'd better make it extra good. The secret to this recipe is a blend of sweet spices and a streusel topping crunchy with nuts and oats.

3 to 4 large sweet-tart apples

½ cup packed dark brown sugar

¾ teaspoon ground cinnamon

¼ teaspoon freshly grated nutmeg

⅛ teaspoon ground cloves

Walnut-Oat Streusel Topping (recipe follows)

Heavy cream or vanilla ice cream (optional)

1. Preheat the oven to 350°F.

2. Peel and slice the apples and measure out 4 heaping cups. Toss the apple slices with the brown sugar, cinnamon, nutmeg, and cloves. Spread out the slices in an even layer in a 9-inch glass pie plate or other 1- to 1½-quart baking dish. Sprinkle the streusel topping over the apples.

3. Bake for 55 to 60 minutes, until the apples are softened and the juices are bubbling. Remove the crisp from the oven and let cool for 15 minutes before serving, with a drizzle of heavy cream or a scoop of ice cream, if desired.

Walnut-Oat Streusel Topping

MAKES ABOUT 1½ CUPS

½ cup unbleached all-purpose flour

½ cup rolled oats

2 tablespoons dark brown sugar

¼ teaspoon ground cinnamon

4 tablespoons cold unsalted butter, cut into small cubes

¼ cup chopped walnuts

Place the flour, oats, brown sugar, and cinnamon in a mixing bowl and rub together with your fingertips to blend and break up any clumps of brown sugar. Scatter the butter cubes over the flour mixture. Continue to rub the ingredients together with your fingertips until it forms small clumps and the butter is no longer visible. Add the walnuts and stir them in. Use immediately or store airtight in the refrigerator for as long as 3 weeks.

It's All in the Name

Words like *crisp, cobbler, buckle, grunt, slump, pandowdy,* and *betty* make a funny group of names for desserts, but they all consist of sweetened and flavored fruit baked under a cloak of crumbs, biscuits, pie crust, or corn bread. While you could write a book about these names, and someone probably has, all of them actually make sense when you stop to think about their structures. *Crisps* cover the fruit with a buttery topping that, with or without nuts, bakes up crunchy. A *cobbler* is cloaked with a layer of biscuits, which suggests a cobblestone road. When baked, the fruit in a *buckle* rises in some spots and sinks in others, giving it a buckled appearance. *Grunts* take their name from the noise the fruit and dumplings make as they simmer on the stovetop—or the sounds hungry eaters make when they scarf down the dessert. *Slump* is merely another name for a grunt. A *pandowdy* may refer to the fact that the fruit dessert is cooked in a pan and is plain in appearance, though not at all in taste. A *betty* refers to the American take on English summer pudding, which sandwiches fruit between layers of bread or crumbs. All these desserts are served warm or at room temperature.

APPLE-GINGERSNAP BROWN BETTY

SERVES 6

Sweetened and spiced apples layered in a dish with crunchy gingersnap cookies and topped with streusel crumbs produce a dessert that is complex in flavor and texture and unbelievably simple to make.

¾ cup sugar

1 tablespoon unbleached all-purpose flour

1½ teaspoons ground cinnamon

½ teaspoon ground cardamom

½ teaspoon freshly grated nutmeg

6 cups sliced, peeled apples (1½ to 2 pounds), preferably Granny Smith

2 cups coarsely broken gingersnap cookies

¼ cup heavy cream

Walnut-Oat Streusel Topping (page 90)

Vanilla ice cream (optional)

1 Preheat the oven to 375°F.

2 In a mixing bowl, combine the sugar, flour, cinnamon, cardamom, and nutmeg. Add the apples and toss gently to coat them with the flour and spices.

3 Arrange half the apple slices in an even layer in an 8-inch square baking dish or other shallow 1½-quart glass or ceramic casserole. Sprinkle half of the gingersnaps over the apples and repeat with another layer of the remaining apples and cookies. Drizzle on the heavy cream and top with the streusel topping.

4 Bake for 45 to 50 minutes, until the apples are tender. Let cool for 15 minutes. Serve warm, with a scoop of ice cream, if desired.

BLACKBERRY COBBLER
WITH CINNAMON-SWIRL BISCUITS

SERVES 8

When Martha Stewart's former assistant held her son's christening dinner at the Loveless, Martha herself chose the menu. This was the dessert she picked, and she was there to sample it. You can be sure the kitchen was buzzing that day—we wanted to make sure everything was perfect!

2 pounds fresh blackberries (about 7 cups)

2 cups sugar

3 tablespoons cornstarch

Zest of 2 medium lemons, grated

1 vanilla bean

2 tablespoons rose water

Cinnamon-Swirl Biscuits (recipe follows)

1 Preheat the oven to 350°F. Rinse the berries and drain well. Place 8 individual 8-ounce ovenproof custard cups or ramekins on a sturdy greased baking sheet.

2 In a large bowl, combine the sugar, cornstarch, and lemon zest. Split the vanilla bean lengthwise and scrape out the seeds with the tip of a knife, adding them to the sugar mixture (reserve the pod for another use). With your fingertips, rub everything together thoroughly to break up the vanilla and disperse the seeds and lemon zest.

3 Add the berries and rose water and toss gently, taking care not to break the berries. Divide the mixture among the 8 custard cups or ramekins. Set an unbaked biscuit on top of the berries in each cup.

4 Bake for 35 minutes, or until the biscuits are golden brown and the berry juices bubble up and drip down the sides of the cups. Remove from the oven and let stand for 15 minutes before serving.

Cinnamon-Swirl Biscuits

MAKES 8

2 cups unbleached all-purpose flour

¼ cup granulated sugar

2 teaspoons baking powder

¼ teaspoon salt

1 stick (4 ounces) cold unsalted butter, cut into small cubes

About ½ cup buttermilk

½ cup packed dark brown sugar

½ teaspoon ground cinnamon

½ teaspoon ground cardamom

1. In a mixing bowl, combine the flour, granulated sugar, baking powder, and salt. Using a pastry blender, a fork, or your fingertips, cut the butter into the flour mixture until it is the size of small peas. Sprinkle ½ cup buttermilk over the mixture and fold together, adding more buttermilk if necessary to make a soft, tender, slightly sticky dough.

2. Turn out the dough onto a floured surface and gently pat into an 8 by 12-inch rectangle. Mix the brown sugar with the cinnamon and cardamom; sprinkle evenly over the surface of the dough. Starting on the long side, roll the dough into a log. Slice into 8 evenly sized 1-inch rounds.

Baking Tip: These cinnamon biscuits, which closely resemble scones, are delicious by themselves with coffee or tea. To bake these separately, arrange about 2 inches apart on a greased baking sheet. Bake in a 375°F oven for 15 to 18 minutes, until the biscuits are golden brown.

BLACKBERRY AND RASPBERRY CRISP WITH PECAN CRUNCH TOPPING

SERVES 6 TO 8

Wild blackberries grow in a tangle all over the South. As the sweet, juicy berries come into season, pair them with ripe red raspberries for a dramatic-looking duo. When these crisps are done, the juices bubble up, and if some drizzles down the side of the dish, so much the better.

1 cup sugar

3 tablespoons cornstarch

2 teaspoons grated orange zest

1 teaspoon ground cinnamon

1/4 teaspoon ground cardamom

1/2 vanilla bean

1 pound blackberries
(about 4 cups)

1 pound raspberries
(about 4 cups)

Pecan Crunch Topping
(recipe follows)

Vanilla or butter pecan
ice cream (optional)

1. Preheat the oven to 400°F. Place 6 to 8 individual 8-ounce ovenproof custard cups, ramekins, or ovenproof soup bowls on a sturdy baking sheet.

2. In a large bowl, combine the sugar, cornstarch, orange zest, cinnamon, and cardamom. Split the vanilla bean lengthwise in half and with the tip of a sharp knife scrape the seeds into the bowl. Rub the ingredients together with your fingertips, to break up the vanilla seeds and blend them evenly. Add the berries and toss gently to combine.

3. Divide the berries among the custard cups, filling each about three-quarters full. Sprinkle the pecan crunch topping over the fruit.

4. Bake for 25 to 30 minutes, or until the juices are bubbling and the topping is browned and crunchy. Let cool for at least 15 minutes. Serve with a scoop of ice cream, if desired.

Baking Tips: Fresh berries are a real treat, but when they're not available, you can still make this dessert by substituting thawed unsweetened frozen berries.

Pecan Crunch Topping

MAKES ABOUT 1½ CUPS

¾ cup unbleached all-purpose flour

½ cup packed dark brown sugar

½ cup chopped pecans

½ teaspoon ground cinnamon

¼ teaspoon baking soda

4 tablespoons cold unsalted butter, cut into small cubes

1. In a medium bowl, combine the flour, brown sugar, pecans, cinnamon, and baking soda. Toss to mix, rubbing the brown sugar with your fingertips to break up any clumps.

2. Add the butter cubes and continue rubbing the ingredients together until evenly mixed. Use immediately or store airtight in the refrigerator for up to 1 week.

Approximately 450,000 customers a year pass through the Loveless's 142-seat restaurant. It's no wonder there's a long line on weekends!

BLUEBERRY SKILLET COBBLER

SERVES 4

Most country cooks know the beauty of serving a cobbler right out of the cast-iron skillet it's cooked in. The pan is perfect for the dessert, because the berries, tossed with sugar, flour, and spices, are stewed first on the stovetop until thickened, so that the biscuits can be dropped onto the hot stewed fruit before the cobbler is slipped into the oven to bake.

1 cup plus 2 tablespoons unbleached all-purpose flour

¾ cup plus 3 tablespoons sugar

1¼ teaspoons baking powder

3 tablespoons cold unsalted butter, cut into small cubes

1 egg, lightly beaten

¼ cup heavy cream

5 cups blueberries

¾ teaspoon grated orange zest

¼ teaspoon ground mace

⅔ cup freshly squeezed orange juice (2 to 3 oranges)

Vanilla or buttermilk ice cream (optional)

1   Preheat the oven to 350°F.

2   In a medium bowl, mix 1 cup of the flour with 3 tablespoons of the sugar and the baking powder. Add the butter and, using your fingertips, rub the butter cubes into the flour until it resembles coarse meal. Add the egg and cream and mix to combine the ingredients evenly and form a soft dough.

3   In a 10-inch cast-iron skillet, combine the blueberries, remaining ¾ cup sugar and 2 tablespoons flour, the orange zest, and the mace. Stir to coat the berries. Pour in the orange juice and set over medium-low heat. Bring the fruit to a boil, reduce the heat, and simmer for 2 minutes to thicken the mixture and cook the flour. Remove the skillet from the heat. Drop rounded tablespoons of the biscuit dough onto the fruit, leaving a little space in between. There should be 12 to 16 biscuits.

4   Place the skillet in the oven and bake for 16 minutes, or until the biscuits are lightly browned on top. Remove from the oven and let stand for 15 to 20 minutes. Serve warm, with a scoop of ice cream, if desired.

MIXED-BERRY GRUNT

SERVES 4

There is some debate over whether a grunt should be cooked covered on the stove to steam the dumplings or placed in the oven to bake them. In this quick and easy version, the berries are simmered on top of the stove in a cast-iron skillet. After a few minutes, biscuit dumplings are dolloped on top and the dessert is then transferred to the oven.

4 cups fresh berries—any combination of blackberries, blueberries, raspberries, and strawberries

1 cup freshly squeezed orange juice

¾ cup sugar

1 inch of vanilla bean, split lengthwise in half

1 teaspoon ground cinnamon

½ teaspoon ground cardamom

Sweet Cream Dumplings (recipe follows)

Vanilla or buttermilk ice cream, for serving

1 Preheat the oven to 350°F.

2 Place the berries in a 10-inch cast-iron skillet. Add the orange juice, sugar, vanilla bean, cinnamon, and cardamom. Bring to a simmer over medium-low heat and cook for 3 to 5 minutes. Remove the vanilla bean.

3 Drop 12 to 14 tablespoon-size dollops of dumpling dough over the top of the fruit, leaving small spaces in between.

4 Bake for 18 minutes, or until the dumplings are lightly browned. Allow the grunt to cool for 15 minutes. To serve, place a scoop of ice cream in a serving dish and top with a portion of fruit and dumplings.

Sweet Cream Dumplings

MAKES 12 TO 14

¾ cup unbleached all-purpose flour

2 tablespoons sugar

1 teaspoon baking powder

2 tablespoons cold unsalted butter, cut into cubes

½ cup heavy cream

Combine the flour, sugar, and baking powder in a mixing bowl. Add the butter cubes and rub together with your fingertips until the mixture resembles coarse meal. Pour in the cream and stir to form a soft dough. Use at once.

PEACH BISCUIT BROWN BETTY

SERVES 4

Traditionally, brown Betty desserts are made with slices of bread or crumbs. We have our own traditions at the Loveless, and when bread is called for we often use leftover biscuits instead. Layers of sweetened and spiced peaches alternated with crumbled biscuits are baked to a puddinglike consistency for the perfect simple dessert, especially if served the way we do—with a dollop of whipped cream and a drizzle of caramel sauce.

²/₃ cup packed light brown sugar

¾ teaspoon ground cinnamon

½ teaspoon freshly grated nutmeg

4 cups sliced peeled peaches (2½ to 3 pounds fresh peaches)

2 cups crumbled biscuits (eight to ten 2-inch biscuits)

⅓ cup freshly squeezed orange juice (about 1 orange)

2 tablespoons unsalted butter, melted

2 tablespoons cinnamon sugar

Whipped cream and Drunken Caramel Sauce (page 206; optional)

1 Preheat the oven to 375°F.

2 In a medium bowl, rub the brown sugar with the cinnamon and nutmeg to combine. Add the peaches and mix gently to coat the peaches with the sugar. Place half of the peaches in the bottom of a buttered 1½-quart baking dish that is at least 2 inches deep. Top with half of the crumbled biscuits. Spoon the remaining peaches over the biscuits and drizzle the orange juice evenly over the dish. Toss the remaining crumbled biscuits with the melted butter and spread over the top of the peaches. Sprinkle liberally with the cinnamon sugar.

3 Bake for 45 minutes, or until the biscuits are an even golden color on top and the juices are bubbly. Let cool for about 15 minutes before serving, with a spoonful of whipped cream and a drizzle of caramel sauce, if you like.

Baking Tip: You could use purchased baking powder biscuits for this recipe or make a half recipe of Sweet Biscuits (page 127).

PEACH COBBLER

SERVES 4

Nothing says "Southern" more than a warm peach cobbler. Choose your fruit carefully, making sure it is slightly soft but not bruised, ripe but still juicy. At the Loveless, we serve cobbler warm with a scoop of ice cream.

2/3 cup granulated sugar

2 tablespoons unbleached all-purpose flour

1 teaspoon grated lemon zest

3/4 teaspoon ground cinnamon

1/2 teaspoon ground mace

4 cups sliced peeled ripe peaches (2½ to 3 pounds fresh peaches)

Sweet Cream Dumplings (page 101)

2 tablespoons cinnamon sugar

1. Preheat the oven to 375°F.

2. In a mixing bowl, stir the granulated sugar, flour, lemon zest, cinnamon, and mace together. Add the peaches and toss gently to coat them with the sugar and spices. Scrape the peach filling into a 1- to 1½-quart casserole. Place the casserole on a sturdy baking sheet.

3. On a floured surface, pat the dumpling dough into a ½-inch-thick slab. Use a 2-inch round cutter to cut it into individual biscuits, reworking the scraps once to make more biscuits.

4. Arrange the biscuits over the top of the peaches. Sprinkle the cinnamon sugar over the biscuits.

5. Bake for 45 to 50 minutes, until the juices are bubbly and the biscuits are golden. Let the cobbler cool for 15 to 20 minutes before serving. Spoon the cobbler into individual dishes, making an effort to divide the biscuits evenly among them.

SPICED PEAR COBBLER WITH BROWN SUGAR SCONES

SERVES 6

The brown sugar topping here is made of scones, but the recipe is tweaked with a bit more liquid so that the dough spreads out nicely when baked on top of the fruit. Cardamom, fresh ginger, and pears make a beautiful trio.

1 cup granulated sugar

3 tablespoons unbleached all-purpose flour

1½ teaspoons grated lemon zest

1 teaspoon grated fresh ginger

½ teaspoon ground cardamom

6 cups sliced peeled ripe pears, preferably Anjou

Brown Sugar Scones (recipe follows)

1 tablespoon coarse sugar

Vanilla ice cream (optional)

1. Preheat the oven to 375°F. Place a 7 by 11-inch baking dish on a sturdy baking sheet.

2. In a bowl, combine the granulated sugar, flour, lemon zest, ginger, and cardamom. Add the pears and toss gently to combine. Scrape the pears into the baking dish. Drop the scones evenly over the fruit, using 2 teaspoons and leaving space in between. Sprinkle the coarse sugar over the cobbler.

3. Bake for 55 minutes, until the juices are bubbly and the biscuits are golden. Let the cobbler cool for 15 to 20 minutes before serving. To serve, spoon out portions into dishes, dividing the scones evenly. Top with a scoop of ice cream, if desired.

Brown Sugar Scones

1 cup unbleached all-purpose flour

¼ cup packed dark brown sugar

1 teaspoon baking powder

4 tablespoons unsalted cold butter, cut into cubes

⅔ cup buttermilk

In a mixing bowl, combine the flour with the brown sugar and baking powder. Add the butter cubes and rub together with your fingertips until the butter bits are smaller than the size of a pea. Sprinkle the buttermilk over the mixture and stir together. Use immediately.

SOUR CHERRY BUCKLE

SERVES 8 TO 10

This delicate almond-flavored cake topped with luscious tart cherries and oat crumb streusel is perfect for any occasion. In the oven, some of the cherries will sink down and allow the cake to bubble up in spots and appear buckled—hence the name. Finding tart cherries can be a challenge unless you have a farmers' market or a tree in your yard. Even then, the season is short, so don't hesitate to use frozen.

2½ cups fresh or frozen (thawed) tart cherries, pitted (about 1 pound)

1⅓ cups sugar

1½ cups plus 2 tablespoons unbleached all-purpose flour

1 stick (4 ounces) unsalted butter, softened

1½ teaspoons almond extract

¼ teaspoon salt

2 eggs

1½ teaspoons baking powder

⅔ cup milk

Walnut-Oat Streusel Topping (page 90)

1. Preheat the oven to 350°F. Grease an 8-inch square baking pan.

2. If using thawed frozen cherries, be sure they are drained well. Place the cherries in a bowl and toss them with ⅓ cup of the sugar and 2 tablespoons of the flour.

3. In a mixing bowl, cream the butter with the remaining 1 cup sugar, the almond extract, and the salt, using an electric mixer on medium speed. Add the eggs, one at a time, scraping the bowl between additions and mixing completely. Sift the remaining 1½ cups flour and the baking powder over the mixture and pour in the milk. Fold the batter by hand. Turn it into the prepared pan. Spoon the cherries and any liquid in the bowl evenly over the batter and top with the streusel topping.

4. Bake for 1 hour to 1 hour and 15 minutes, or until a toothpick or cake tester inserted in the center comes out clean. Serve warm or at room temperature.

BLUEBERRY PEACH CORN BREAD BUCKLE

SERVES 6 TO 8

At the cafe, we showcase the duo of blueberries and peaches in cobblers, pies, tarts, and muffins. White cornmeal in a lightly sweetened cake contrasts nicely with the flavors of the fruit and the crumb topping. During baking, the layers rise in some spots and sink in others to leave the fruit in random pockets, thus giving it a buckled appearance and its name.

1½ cups blueberries

1½ cups diced (½ inch) peeled peaches

1 cup sugar

1½ teaspoons grated lemon zest

⅔ cup cornmeal, preferably white

1 cup unbleached all-purpose flour

1 tablespoon baking powder

¼ teaspoon salt

⅓ cup canola or other neutral vegetable oil

1 egg, lightly beaten

¾ cup buttermilk

1 cup Brown Sugar and Oat Crumb Topping (page 7)

Sweetened Whipped Cream (optional; page 19)

1. Preheat the oven to 350°F. Grease and flour a 9-inch round cake pan.

2. In a medium bowl, combine the blueberries, peaches, ⅓ cup of the sugar, and the lemon zest. Toss gently to coat the fruit with the sugar. Let it macerate while you prepare the cornmeal cake.

3. In another bowl, stir together the cornmeal, flour, baking powder, and salt with the remaining ⅔ cup sugar. Pour in the oil, egg, and buttermilk and stir until smooth. Scrape the batter into the prepared cake pan. Arrange the fruits and their juices evenly over the top of the cake. Sprinkle the crumb topping evenly over the fruit.

4. Bake for 1 hour and 15 minutes, or until a toothpick or cake tester inserted in the center comes out clean. Let the cake cool in the pan for 15 minutes; then invert it onto a flat tray. Place another tray on the cake and invert it again right side up. Cut the cake into wedges and serve warm with a dollop of whipped cream, if desired.

Blueberry Peach Corn Bread Buckle (left)
and Raspberry Plum Pandowdy (right, page 110)

RASPBERRY PLUM PANDOWDY

SERVES 4 TO 6

This recipe makes excellent use of black plums, which are not as commonly used for cooking. The contrast of their pitch-dark skin and deep red flesh makes beautiful tarts, pies, cobblers, and, of course, pandowdies.

¾ cup granulated sugar

2 tablespoons unbleached all-purpose flour

1 teaspoon grated fresh ginger

1 teaspoon grated orange zest

Seeds from ¼ vanilla bean

2 cups fresh raspberries

2 cups sliced black plums (6 to 8 medium plums)

½ recipe Flaky Pie Dough (page 48)

Egg wash: 1 egg yolk, beaten with 2 tablespoons water

2 tablespoons coarse sugar

Whipped cream (optional)

1. Preheat the oven to 350°F. Place an 8-inch square glass baking dish on a sturdy baking sheet.

2. In a bowl, rub the granulated sugar, flour, ginger, orange zest, and vanilla seeds together with your fingertips to combine them. Add the raspberries and plums and toss gently to coat the fruit with the sugar mixture. Scrape the fruit into the baking dish in a level layer.

3. Roll out the dough to an 8-inch square on a floured surface. Carefully transfer the dough to the baking dish and lay it over the fruit to cover it completely. Brush the dough with the egg wash and sprinkle with the coarse sugar.

4. Bake for 40 minutes. Remove the dish from the oven to "dowdy" the crust. To do this, take a large metal spoon and, using its edge, make several cuts, at the same time pressing the dough down into the fruit.

5. Return the dish to the oven and continue baking for 10 to 15 minutes, until the dough is golden and the juices are bubbling. Let the pandowdy cool for 15 to 20 minutes before serving, with a dollop of whipped cream, if desired.

Photograph on page 109.

Shortcakes

Unlike baked fruit desserts, shortcakes layer fresh fruit with cake, biscuits, or cookies, and they are always served chilled or at room temperature. With a shortcake, the cream or ice cream is not an optional garnish but an integral part of the assembled dessert. Because the fruit is presented so starkly, ripeness and quality are especially important, and the desserts are best made when the particular fruit is in high season.

ANGEL BERRY-RHUBARB SHORTCAKE

SERVES 8

Light is a relative term when you're talking about whipping up 1½ cups of heavy cream and embellishing the dessert with a scoop of ice cream. Be that as it may, angel food cake is made with egg whites only and no added fat, so maybe everything balances out.

2 cups rhubarb in ½-inch pieces

2 cups halved strawberries, plus 8 halved strawberries for garnish

⅔ cup plus 2 tablespoons sugar

⅔ cup freshly squeezed orange juice (2 to 3 oranges)

½ teaspoon ground cinnamon

1 inch of vanilla bean, split lengthwise in half

1½ cups heavy cream

¼ teaspoon vanilla extract

Pastel Angel Food Cake (page 84) or a store-bought 10-inch plain cake

1½ pints vanilla or strawberry ice cream

1. Place the rhubarb and 2 cups of the strawberries in a nonreactive saucepan with ⅔ cup of the sugar, the orange juice, cinnamon, and vanilla bean. Simmer over medium-low heat until the rhubarb is tender, 15 to 20 minutes. Remove the vanilla bean. Let the fruit compote cool slightly, then cover and refrigerate until chilled completely, about 2 hours.

2. Shortly before serving, whip the heavy cream in a chilled bowl with chilled beaters until it thickens. Beat in the remaining 2 tablespoons sugar and the vanilla extract and whip until the cream is fairly stiff but still spreads slightly when spooned out.

3. To assemble the dessert, cut the angel food cake into 8 generous wedges. Place a slice of cake on each of 8 dessert plates. Place a scoop of ice cream on each slice and top with a large spoonful of the berry-rhubarb compote. Garnish with a dollop of whipped cream and the halved strawberries, arranging them cut sides up.

Photograph on page 87.

Baking Tip: This recipe uses just a little bit of vanilla bean, so it's the perfect opportunity to recycle a pod you've already scraped clean. If you don't have a piece of vanilla bean lying around, you may substitute ½ teaspoon vanilla extract.

BLACKBERRY PLUM SHORTCAKES WITH LEMON CREAM

SERVES 6

Don't get overly excited: The biscuit recipe used to make these shortcakes is *not* for the famous Loveless biscuits. That recipe is a secret; this one is all yours. Because only 3 tablespoons of lemon curd go into the lemon cream, you can use a quality prepared brand to save time.

Lemon Cream (recipe follows)

Buttermilk Biscuits
(recipe follows)

2 cups sliced black plums
(6 to 8 medium plums)

1½ cups blackberries

1 tablespoon freshly squeezed lemon juice

½ cup sugar

1 inch of vanilla bean,
split lengthwise in half

1 teaspoon grated lemon zest

Lemon balm or lemon verbena leaves for garnish

1. Make the lemon cream and refrigerate.

2. Bake the buttermilk biscuits as directed and let them cool. Split the biscuits in half with a fork or a serrated knife.

3. Toss the plums and berries with the lemon juice. Place the sugar in a small bowl, scrape the vanilla seeds into the sugar with the tip of a sharp knife, add the zest, and rub the ingredients together to blend them. Toss the fruit with the sugar mixture and macerate for 1 hour.

4. To assemble the dessert, place the bottom halves of 6 biscuits onto 6 dessert plates. Spoon the fruit and juices onto the biscuits. Top with a dollop of lemon cream. Finish the dessert off by placing the top halves of each biscuit over the cream, slightly askew. Garnish with a sprig of lemon balm or lemon verbena leaves.

Lemon Cream

MAKES ABOUT 3 CUPS

1½ cups heavy cream

2 tablespoons sugar

3 tablespoons Lemon Curd
(page 121) or store-bought

Whip the cream with the sugar until slightly stiff peaks form. Fold the lemon curd into the cream by hand until just blended. Cover and refrigerate for up to 2 hours before using.

Buttermilk Biscuits

MAKES TEN TO TWELVE 3-INCH BISCUITS

3½ cups unbleached
all-purpose flour

1 tablespoon plus 1 teaspoon
baking powder

1 teaspoon baking soda

1 teaspoon salt

1 stick (4 ounces) plus
2 tablespoons unsalted
cold butter, cut into cubes

1½ cups buttermilk

1. Preheat the oven to 425°F. Line a sturdy baking sheet with parchment paper.

2. Combine the flour, baking powder, baking soda, salt, and butter in a food processor. Pulse until the butter is cut into small pieces no larger than the size of peas. Pour in the buttermilk and pulse just enough to make a smooth dough.

3. Scrape the dough out onto a floured surface. Using your hands, pat into a ½-inch-thick slab. Cut out the biscuits using a 3-inch round cutter and place them on the lined baking sheet; rework the scraps once to make more biscuits.

4. Bake for 12 to 14 minutes, until golden brown. Let cool completely and then use at once. Choose the 6 nicest-looking biscuits for the shortcake. Save the others for a snack.

BANANAS FOSTER SHORTCAKE

SERVES 6

Bananas Foster hails from Brennan's restaurant in New Orleans, but it's enjoyed all over the country, and here in Tennessee we love bananas in all kinds of desserts. At the Loveless, we omit the banana liqueur found in bananas Foster and add Chinese five-spice powder. Keep in mind that while all the components can be prepared in advance, the individual portions should be assembled just before serving.

Brown Sugar Buttermilk Pound Cake (page 135)

3 cups ¼-inch-thick banana slices (4 to 5 bananas)

2 tablespoons freshly squeezed lemon juice

1 cup packed dark brown sugar

1 teaspoon Chinese five-spice powder or ground cinnamon

1 inch of vanilla bean, split lengthwise in half

2 tablespoons dark rum

1 pint vanilla or butter pecan ice cream

1. Trim the short ends off the pound cake and slice the remaining cake into 6 equal slabs.

2. In a medium bowl, toss the bananas with the lemon juice; set aside. Place the brown sugar, five-spice powder, vanilla bean, and 2 tablespoons water in a small heavy saucepan and bring to a boil over medium-low heat. Boil for a minute or two to infuse the flavors; remove from the heat and let cool for at least 5 minutes. Remove the vanilla bean.

3. When you're ready to serve dessert, assemble the shortcakes: Place a slice of cake on each of 6 serving plates. Warm the syrup slightly, if necessary; remove from the heat and stir in the rum. Top each slice of pound cake with a rounded scoop of ice cream. Pour the syrup over the banana slices and spoon the bananas and syrup over the ice cream and cake. Serve at once.

FOURTH OF JULY BERRY SHORTCAKES WITH BUTTERMILK BISCUITS

SERVES 6

As you might imagine, Fourth of July in this all-American rootin'-tootin' music-lovin' country town is a very loud holiday. Nashville celebrates with a huge fireworks display on the river downtown, and many families fill up at the Loveless Cafe before heading on to the holiday festivities.

Buttermilk Biscuits (page 115)

½ cup plus 2 tablespoons sugar

1 inch of vanilla bean, split lengthwise in half

½ teaspoon grated orange zest

3 cups mixed fresh berries, such as strawberries, raspberries, blueberries, and blackberries

1½ cups heavy cream

½ teaspoon vanilla extract

Whole berries and fresh mint sprigs for garnish

1 Split the biscuits horizontally with a fork or a knife.

2 Place ½ cup of the sugar in a small bowl, scrape the vanilla seeds into the sugar with the tip of a sharp knife, add the zest, and rub the ingredients together to blend them. Add the berries, toss gently, and let the fruit macerate at room temperature for about an hour.

3 In a chilled bowl with chilled beaters, whip the cream with the remaining 2 tablespoons sugar and the vanilla extract until the cream mounds softly.

4 To assemble the shortcakes, place the bottoms of the biscuits on 6 dessert plates. Ladle the macerated berries with their syrup over the biscuit bottoms so that they spill over onto the plate. Drop generous dollops of whipped cream onto the berries and finish it all off with the biscuit tops. Garnish each with a few whole berries and a sprig of mint.

BLUEBERRY LEMON SHORTCAKE WITH OAT SCONES

SERVES 8

These scones are good by themselves, so imagine them heaped with lemony blueberries and filled with tart lemon curd, a marriage that's made in heaven to begin with.

4 cups fresh blueberries

1 cup plus 1 tablespoon sugar

2 teaspoons grated lemon zest

2 teaspoons rose water

1 teaspoon grated fresh ginger

1 inch of vanilla bean, split lengthwise in half

1 cup heavy cream

1/4 teaspoon vanilla extract

Oat Scones (recipe follows)

1 1/4 cups Lemon Curd (recipe follows)

1 Place 2 cups of the blueberries in a medium nonreactive saucepan with 1/2 cup of the sugar and 1 teaspoon of the lemon zest. Bring to a simmer over low heat. Cook for 3 to 5 minutes, until the berries burst. Press the mixture through a food mill or strainer to extract as much of the juice as possible while straining out the skins. Stir in the rose water and refrigerate until completely chilled, about 2 hours.

2 Shortly before serving dessert, toss the remaining 2 cups blueberries with 1/2 cup of the remaining sugar, the remaining 1 teaspoon lemon zest, the ginger, and the vanilla seeds scraped from the bean with the tip of a sharp knife. Let macerate for 10 to 15 minutes. Meanwhile, in a chilled bowl with chilled beaters, whip the cream with the remaining 1 tablespoon sugar and the vanilla extract until soft peaks form.

3 To assemble the shortcakes, split the scones horizontally and place the bottoms on 8 dessert plates. Spoon a generous dollop of lemon curd onto each of the scones. Top with the blueberries and any juices in the bowl and cover with the top halves of the scones. Drizzle the chilled blueberry sauce around the plates and garnish with the whipped cream.

Oat Scones

MAKES 8 SCONES

1¾ cups unbleached
all-purpose flour

½ cup rolled oats

¼ cup packed dark brown sugar

2 teaspoons baking powder

½ teaspoon ground cinnamon

½ teaspoon salt

1 stick (4 ounces) cold unsalted
butter, cut into cubes

⅔ cup buttermilk

2 tablespoons cinnamon sugar

1. Preheat the oven to 425°F. Line a baking sheet with parchment paper or a silicone liner.

2. In a mixing bowl, stir together the flour, oats, brown sugar, baking powder, cinnamon, and salt. Cut in the butter with a fork, a pastry blender, or your fingertips until the butter is the size of small peas. Sprinkle the buttermilk over the mixture and stir together to form a soft dough.

3. On a floured surface, pat the dough into a thick, round disk about 7 inches in diameter. Using a sharp knife, cut the disk like a pie into 8 equal wedges. Place the scones on the lined sheet about 2 inches apart. Dust with the cinnamon sugar.

4. Bake for 12 to 14 minutes, until the scones are golden on the bottom and firm when touched. Transfer to a rack to cool.

Lemon Curd

MAKES ABOUT 1¼ CUPS

6 egg yolks

¾ cup sugar

¼ cup plus 2 tablespoons
freshly squeezed lemon juice

1 tablespoon grated lemon zest

Whisk the egg yolks with the sugar in a small nonreactive saucepan. Add the juice and zest and whisk to combine. Cook the mixture over low heat, stirring gently, until it coats the spoon, 5 to 10 minutes. Do not let it boil or the eggs will curdle. Strain the curd, press plastic wrap directly onto the surface, and refrigerate the mixture until thoroughly chilled.

FRUIT SUNDAE CREAM PUFFS

SERVES 8

Here's the Loveless country version of French profiteroles, dressed up with fresh fruit as well as ice cream and chocolate sauce. This is not a true shortcake, but it serves much the same purpose: a vehicle for presenting fresh fruit with plenty of whipped cream.

8 Cream Puff Shells
(page 124)

1 quart vanilla ice cream

3 cups mixed fresh fruit, such as bananas, pineapple, and strawberries, cut into 1/4-inch-thick pieces

1/4 cup plus 1 tablespoon sugar

1 1/2 cups heavy cream

1/4 teaspoon vanilla extract

Chocolate Sauce
(page 124)

1. Slice the tops off the cooled cream puffs, about 1/2 inch from the highest point on the puff, and set aside. Remove and discard any soft eggy parts in the center.

2. About 20 minutes before serving, let the ice cream soften and make 8 round scoops. Place the scoops in the bottom of the pastry shells set on a small tray and freeze while you prepare the remaining components.

3. Place the fruit slices in a bowl and toss with 3 tablespoons of the sugar.

4. In a chilled bowl with chilled beaters, whip the cream with the remaining 2 tablespoons sugar and the vanilla until soft peaks form.

5. To assemble the dessert, place the ice-cream-filled cream puffs on individual dessert plates. Divide the sweetened fruit among the 8 puffs. Drizzle the chocolate sauce over the puffs as well as a little around each of the plates. Top with a dollop of whipped cream and place the top of the puff on it like a little hat. Serve immediately.

Cream Puff Shells

MAKES 10 LARGE PUFFS

1 stick (4 ounces) unsalted butter

½ teaspoon salt

1 cup unbleached all-purpose flour

4 eggs

Baking Tip: This recipe makes 10 puffs, and you need only 8 for the Fruit Sundae Cream Puffs, so pick the best-shaped ones. Use the other two in the next couple of days or freeze and pull out anytime you need a last-minute dessert for two.

1. Preheat the oven to 400°F. Line a baking sheet with parchment paper or a silicone liner.

2. Place the butter, 1 cup water, and the salt in a heavy medium saucepan over low heat. When the butter is melted, raise the heat to medium and bring to a boil. Add the flour all at once and stir vigorously with a wooden spoon until evenly blended. Return to medium-low heat and continue to cook the flour paste for several minutes (it should resemble mashed potatoes), until it begins to stick to the bottom of the pan.

3. Scrape the paste into a large mixing bowl and beat with an electric mixer on medium speed for 1 minute to cool slightly. Add the eggs, one at a time, beating until thoroughly incorporated and scraping the bowl after each addition. When the mixture is completely smooth, scoop up the puff paste with a ¼-cup measure and place on the lined baking sheet about 2½ inches apart.

4. Bake for 20 minutes, then reduce the oven temperature to 350°F and bake for another 20 minutes. If you see any trace of yellow in the cracks of the puffs, bake for 3 to 5 minutes longer; otherwise they will collapse as they cool. Transfer to a rack to cool.

Chocolate Sauce

MAKES ABOUT 1 CUP

6 ounces semisweet chocolate, chopped

¼ cup plus 2 tablespoons half-and-half

Place the chocolate and half-and-half in a microwave-safe bowl and warm on the lowest heat setting or the defrost setting for 1½ minutes. Remove and stir. Continue to heat in 30-second intervals and stir until the chocolate is melted and the sauce is smooth. Keep warm until ready to use.

KENTUCKY BOURBON PEACH SHORTCAKE

SERVES 8

Kentucky is only a stone's throw away from Tennessee. The two states kiss along our northern border. So it's no surprise that next to our own distilled whiskey—one step away from moonshine—the favorite hard liquor around these parts is bourbon.

⅔ cup sugar

1 inch of vanilla bean, split lengthwise in half

¼ teaspoon ground cardamom

¼ teaspoon ground cinnamon

Pinch of grated lemon zest

4 cups sliced fresh peaches, peeled if desired (2½ to 3 pounds fresh peaches)

2 tablespoons freshly squeezed lemon juice

Brown Sugar Buttermilk Pound Cake (page 135) or store-bought pound cake

1 quart butter pecan ice cream

Drunken Caramel Sauce (page 206), made with Kentucky bourbon

Fresh mint sprigs for garnish

1 Place the sugar in a bowl and add the vanilla seeds scraped from the bean with the tip of a sharp knife, the cardamom, cinnamon, and lemon zest; rub together with your fingertips to blend evenly. Add the peach slices and lemon juice and toss gently to coat. Let the peaches macerate at room temperature for at least 20 minutes.

2 To assemble the shortcakes, cut the pound cake into slices about ¾ inch thick. Place a slice on each of 8 dessert plates. Moisten the cake with some of the juices from the bowl of peaches. Top with a scoop of ice cream. Spoon the peach slices and remaining juices around the cake. Using a small pitcher, drizzle the caramel sauce over the ice cream and peaches in a thin stream. Garnish each shortcake with a sprig of mint.

RASPBERRY PEACH SHORTCAKE WITH SWEET BISCUITS

SERVES 6

Rose water, our favorite secret ingredient for red berries, is easy to find and brings out the essence of the fruit. Again, this is not the recipe for the famous Loveless biscuits either, but these are delicious in their own right.

Sweet Biscuits (recipe follows)

⅓ cup plus 2 tablespoons sugar

½ teaspoon grated orange zest

2 teaspoons rose water

1 inch of vanilla bean, split lengthwise in half

2 cups sliced peeled peaches (1½ to 2 pounds fresh peaches)

1½ cups heavy cream

¼ teaspoon vanilla extract

1½ cups fresh raspberries

Edible flowers for garnish (optional)

1 Split 6 biscuits horizontally with a fork or a knife.

2 In a bowl, combine ⅓ cup of the sugar with the orange zest and rose water. With the tip of a small knife, scrape out the seeds of the vanilla bean and add to the sugar. Rub with your fingertips to blend. Add the peaches and toss gently. Allow the peaches to macerate for about 1 hour.

3 Shortly before serving, in a chilled bowl with chilled beaters, whip the cream with the remaining 2 tablespoons sugar and the vanilla extract until soft peaks form.

4 To assemble the shortcakes, place the bottoms of the biscuits on each of 6 dessert plates. Spoon the peaches and any syrup in the bowl over the biscuit bottoms. Add ¼ cup raspberries to each. Top with a generous dollop of the whipped cream and finish them off with the biscuit tops. Garnish with a small rosebud or other edible flower, if you wish.

Sweet Biscuits

4 cups unbleached all-purpose flour

²/₃ cup granulated sugar

2 tablespoons baking powder

½ teaspoon salt

1 stick (4 ounces) cold unsalted butter, cut into cubes

2 cups heavy cream

Coarse sugar

1 Preheat the oven to 425°F. Line a baking sheet with parchment paper or a silicone mat.

2 Place the flour, granulated sugar, baking powder, and salt in a bowl and stir to combine. Sprinkle the butter cubes over the flour and cut them in using 2 knives, a pastry blender, or your fingertips until the mixture resembles coarse meal.

3 Drizzle the cream around the bowl and stir to form a soft dough. Scrape the dough out onto a floured surface and pat it into a ½-inch-thick slab. Use a 3-inch round cutter to cut the biscuits and place them about 2 inches apart on the prepared pan. Rework the scraps once to make more biscuits. Sprinkle the tops with coarse sugar.

4 Bake for 14 minutes, or until the biscuits are golden brown. Transfer to a wire rack to cool completely before using.

Every week the Loveless uses 1,500 pounds of flour to make biscuits—that's three-quarters of a ton! We also sell about 250 of our 2-pound bags of Loveless Biscuit Mix every week at Hams & Jams and through our mail-order catalog. While the recipe for our famous homemade biscuits is never divulged, fans can come close with our signature mix.

CHOCOLATE RASPBERRY SHORT STACKS

SERVES 6

Here is a made-from-scratch version of an old back-of-the-box classic, popular in the South, which layers chocolate wafers and whipped cream. This recipe makes individual stacks, using whipped cream flavored with chocolate, and adding fresh raspberries as well as a raspberry sauce.

12 ounces frozen raspberries, thawed, with their juices

⅓ cup sugar

½ teaspoon grated orange zest

1 inch of vanilla bean, split lengthwise in half

2 teaspoons rose water

4 ounces semisweet chocolate, chopped

1½ cups heavy cream

18 chocolate wafers, homemade (see page 174) or store-bought

2 to 3 cups fresh raspberries

Sweetened Whipped Cream (page 19) and chocolate shavings for garnish

1. Place the defrosted berries and their juices in a small nonreactive saucepan with the sugar, orange zest, and vanilla bean. Simmer over low heat for 5 minutes, stirring occasionally. Pour into a strainer set over a bowl and press the berries gently to extract as much of their juice as possible without pushing the seeds through. Stir in the rose water, cover, and refrigerate the raspberry sauce until chilled, about 2 hours.

2. To prepare the chocolate whipped cream, place the chocolate and ½ cup of the heavy cream in a heatproof bowl. Set over (not in) a pan of barely simmering water and warm, stirring occasionally, until the chocolate melts. Remove from the heat and let cool until tepid. Whip the remaining 1 cup cream to soft peaks in a chilled bowl with chilled beaters. Fold the whipped cream into the chocolate mixture gently just until no streaks remain.

3. To assemble the stacks, place one chocolate wafer on each of 6 dessert plates. Using a piping bag or a large spoon, dollop a heaping tablespoon of chocolate cream onto each cookie and top with a few fresh raspberries. Repeat with another chocolate wafer, more chocolate cream, and a few more berries. Top each stack with a final chocolate wafer, pressing gently in the center so the cookie adheres. To garnish, add a small dollop of whipped cream and some chocolate shavings. Drizzle a tablespoon or two of the raspberry sauce around the plate.

CHAPTER 4

Coffee Cakes, Tea Cakes, and Cheesecakes

Marbled Sour Cream Pound Cake (page 137)

When traveling to small towns

in Tennessee, it's not uncommon to find tearooms that anchor the neat village squares. As much as they speak to the gentility of ladies gathering for lunch, they also remind us that we enjoy eating at times other than at the three principal meals. Tearooms also prove that desserts do not only serve to signal the end of a meal. Some sweets have a higher calling, deserve to be the center of attention, and are a respite unto themselves.

Though no one has ever confused the Loveless Cafe with a tearoom, there are some similarities. Both feature dessert as the star attraction, plus people do like to stop and have a sweet bite at the Loveless all throughout the day. They especially enjoy having a quiet moment in the midafternoon for their own personal coffee or tea break whether in work attire or jeans and boots.

There's really no stark dividing line on the dessert continuum that separates coffee cakes from tea cakes, though both are usually simpler than a frosted layer cake. What unites them is that they are both good at any time of day, and most tend to fall into the simple quick bread category. Of course, they're best eaten

with whatever you choose to sip on. Our Brown Sugar Buttermilk Pound Cake will taste great whether you're drinking a mug of hot coffee, some sweet iced tea, or even a late-night brew.

As much as we make fun of them, fruitcakes also continue to find soft spots in our collective appetites. We're not talking about the sad, dry loaves that call to mind holiday re-gifting. We assure you that with the bourbon-macerated raisins and a final brush of bourbon on the cake, our Tipsy Cake and its chocolate variation won't leave a dry mouth in the house.

For good measure, we throw in a triumvirate of Southern takes on cheesecakes, along with some surefire techniques that help ensure those cakes come out of the oven smooth and silky every time.

BANANA NUT TEA BREAD

MAKES A 9-INCH LOAF; SERVES 6 TO 8

With banana pudding a Southern staple on our dessert menu, we always have bananas on hand at the cafe. They turn up in pancakes and waffles as well as in cakes and this wonderful tea bread. The addition of honey, butter, and sour cream distinguishes this luscious light loaf.

1/3 cup walnuts or pecans

6 tablespoons unsalted butter, softened

3/4 cup sugar

2 tablespoons honey

1/4 teaspoon salt

1 egg

3/4 cup mashed ripe banana (about 2 medium bananas)

1 2/3 cups unbleached all-purpose flour

1 1/4 teaspoons ground cinnamon

3/4 teaspoon baking soda

1/2 cup sour cream

1 Preheat the oven to 350°F. Grease and flour a 9 by 5 by 3-inch loaf pan. Place the nuts in a small baking dish and toast in the oven until fragrant, 5 to 7 minutes. Let cool; then coarsely chop.

2 In a mixing bowl, cream the butter, sugar, honey, and salt until light and fluffy. Scrape the bowl, add the egg, and beat well. Add the mashed bananas and toasted nuts and mix together.

3 Sift the flour, cinnamon, and baking soda over the batter. Fold in the flour a few times by hand with a rubber spatula. Add the sour cream and fold together until the batter is blended evenly. Scrape the batter into the prepared loaf pan.

4 Bake for 1 hour, or until a toothpick or cake tester inserted in the center comes out clean. Let the loaf cool in the pan for 10 minutes; then turn out onto a rack to cool completely.

BROWN SUGAR BUTTERMILK POUND CAKE

MAKES A 9-INCH LOAF; SERVES 8

Annie Loveless, the wife of the original owner of the cafe, had a recipe for brown sugar pound cake that her grandson passed along to us. It's the inspiration for this recipe, which includes buttermilk for a rich, nutty flavor.

1 stick (4 ounces) unsalted butter, softened

1 cup packed dark brown sugar

1 teaspoon vanilla extract

2 whole eggs plus 2 egg yolks

1½ cups cake flour

⅓ cup buttermilk

1 Preheat the oven to 325°F. Grease a 9 by 5 by 3-inch loaf pan, line the bottom with parchment paper, and grease the paper.

2 In a mixing bowl, cream the butter until soft and fluffy. Beat in the brown sugar and vanilla. Continue mixing on medium speed until thoroughly blended. Add the whole eggs and egg yolks one at a time. Mix in each completely and scrape the bowl before adding the next one. Continue to beat on medium speed until light and fluffy.

3 Sift the cake flour directly over the butter mixture. Start to fold it in with a few strokes, then sprinkle the buttermilk evenly over the batter. Finish folding together until blended. Pour the batter into the pan.

4 Bake for 55 to 60 minutes, or until a toothpick or cake tester inserted into the center comes out clean. Let cool in the pan for 10 minutes, then turn out, peel off the paper, and let cool completely on a rack.

Baking Tip: The only leavening agent in a pound cake is the air whipped into the batter. For this reason it's extremely important to add the eggs gradually, one at a time. If they are dumped in all at once, they will break the structure and deflate the batter, resulting in a heavy, dense cake.

FRESH LEMON POUND CAKE

MAKES THREE 5-INCH LOAVES; SERVES 2 TO 3 EACH

This classic cake is rich and lemony and makes a great gift. We offer a number of our pound cakes in small loaf pans to take home or give to others. This one is particularly good with strawberries and whipped cream.

1¾ sticks (7 ounces) unsalted butter, softened

1¾ cups sugar

Grated zest of 3 lemons

3 whole eggs plus 3 egg yolks

2¼ cups unbleached all-purpose flour

¼ teaspoon baking soda

½ cup buttermilk

1. Preheat the oven to 350°F. Grease 3 small loaf pans, 5 by 3 by 2 inches each. Line the bottoms with parchment paper and grease the paper.

2. In a mixing bowl, cream the butter with the sugar and lemon zest until light and fluffy. Add the whole eggs and egg yolks in two or three additions, scraping the sides of the bowl well and mixing completely after each addition. Sift the flour and baking soda over the bowl, pour in the buttermilk, and fold together by hand. Divide the batter among the loaf pans.

3. Bake for about 45 minutes, or until a toothpick or cake tester inserted in the center of a cake comes out clean. Let the cakes stand in their pans for about 5 minutes. Turn them out onto a wire rack, peel off the paper, and let cool completely before slicing.

MARBLED SOUR CREAM POUND CAKE

MAKES TWO 8-INCH LOAVES; SERVES 6 EACH

Marbling is the perfect solution for people who can't decide if they like chocolate or vanilla better, and we sell tons of marbled pound cake at the Loveless.

1¾ sticks (7 ounces) unsalted butter, softened

1¾ cups sugar

2 teaspoons vanilla extract

3 whole eggs plus 3 egg yolks

2¼ cups unbleached all-purpose flour

¼ teaspoon baking soda

⅔ cup sour cream

3 ounces semisweet or bittersweet chocolate, melted and slightly cooled (see page 36)

1. Preheat the oven to 350°F. Grease two 8 by 4 by 2-inch loaf pans. Line the bottoms with parchment paper and grease the paper.

2. In a mixing bowl, cream the butter with the sugar and vanilla until light and fluffy. Add the whole eggs and egg yolks in two or three additions, scraping well and mixing completely after each addition. Sift the flour and baking soda onto the egg mixture, add the sour cream, and fold by hand with a rubber spatula until the batter is evenly blended.

3. Measure out 2 cups of the batter into another bowl. Add the melted chocolate and stir to mix. Place 1 cup of the vanilla batter in each of the loaf pans, spreading it out over the bottom; reserve the remaining batter. Top the vanilla batter in the pans with dollops of the chocolate batter, using about two-thirds of what you have. Divide the remaining vanilla batter between the pans and then top with the remaining chocolate batter. Snake a blunt knife through the pan to swirl the batters together to create a marbled effect.

4. Bake for about 45 minutes, or until a toothpick or cake tester inserted in the center of a cake comes out clean. Let the cakes stand in their pans for about 5 minutes, then turn them out onto a wire rack, peel off the paper, and cool completely.

Photograph on page 131.

MOCHA POUND CAKE

MAKES THREE 5-INCH LOAVES; SERVES 2 TO 3 EACH

To get the most intense mocha flavor in this pound cake, use a good-quality cocoa powder and freshly ground coffee of the darkest roast available.

2 sticks (8 ounces) unsalted butter, softened

2 cups sugar

2 tablespoons freshly ground dark roast coffee beans

1 teaspoon vanilla extract

¼ teaspoon salt

3 whole eggs plus 3 egg yolks

1½ cups cake flour

⅔ cup unsweetened cocoa powder (*not* Dutch process)

⅔ cup sour cream

1. Preheat the oven to 350°F. Grease 3 small loaf pans, 5 by 3 by 2 inches. Line the bottoms with parchment paper and grease the paper.

2. In a mixing bowl, cream the butter with the sugar, coffee, vanilla, and salt until light and fluffy. Add the whole eggs and egg yolks gradually, beating and scraping the bowl between additions to blend well.

3. Sift the cake flour and cocoa over the top of the batter. Fold just a few times, then add the sour cream and fold everything together until no streaks remain. Divide the batter evenly among the 3 prepared pans; there will be about 1½ cups batter for each.

4. Bake for about 1 hour, or until a toothpick or cake tester inserted in the center of a cake comes out clean. Let the cakes stand in the pans for 5 to 10 minutes before inverting and removing them from the pans. Peel off the paper and let the cakes cool completely on a rack before slicing.

VANILLA BEAN POUND CAKE

MAKES A 9-INCH LOAF; SERVES 8

There's no substitute for the rich flavor of real vanilla beans. Even pure extract is not quite the same. This lovely plain cake is perfect just as it is with a cup of tea or used in place of biscuits for a fruit shortcake.

1 stick (4 ounces) plus
1 tablespoon unsalted butter, softened

1 cup sugar

¼ teaspoon salt

½ vanilla bean, split lengthwise in half

2 whole eggs plus 2 egg yolks

1½ cups cake flour

⅓ cup buttermilk

1. Preheat the oven to 325°F. Grease a 9 by 5 by 3-inch loaf pan. Line the bottom with parchment paper and grease the paper.

2. In a mixing bowl, combine the butter with the sugar and salt. With the tip of a knife, scrape the vanilla seeds into the bowl and beat the mixture until light and fluffy. Add the eggs and egg yolks one at a time, scraping the bowl after each addition.

3. Sift the flour over the butter and egg mixture. Fold a few times by hand. Sprinkle the buttermilk over the batter and fold it all in gently. Scrape the batter into the prepared pan.

4. Bake for 55 to 60 minutes, or until a toothpick or cake tester inserted in the center comes out clean. Let the cake stand in the pan for 5 to 10 minutes. Then unmold, peel off the paper, and let the cake cool completely on a rack.

CHERRY CHEESE COFFEE CAKE

MAKES A 10-INCH COFFEE CAKE; SERVES 6

No yeast, no rolling, no waiting—this is simply a delectable easy cake you can whip up in minutes. At the cafe it's one of our most popular breakfast sweets. At home, serve it for brunch with big mugs of strong coffee or in the afternoon with a tall glass of sweet tea.

CAKE

6 tablespoons unsalted butter, softened

2/3 cup sugar

1 teaspoon vanilla extract

1 egg

1 cup unbleached all-purpose flour

3/4 teaspoon baking powder

TOPPING

4 ounces Neufchâtel cheese (reduced-fat cream cheese; do not use fat-free), softened

2 tablespoons unbleached all-purpose flour

4 tablespoons sugar

1/2 teaspoon grated lemon zest

1 egg yolk

1 cup tart cherries, thawed frozen or well-drained canned

1/2 teaspoon almond extract

1/4 teaspoon ground cinnamon

1. Preheat the oven to 375°F. Grease the bottom and sides of a 10-inch springform pan. Line the bottom with a round of parchment paper or wax paper.

2. Make the cake: In a mixing bowl, cream the butter, sugar, and vanilla with an electric mixer on medium speed until fluffy. Add the egg and mix in thoroughly; scrape down the bowl. Add the flour and baking powder and mix only until the flour is incorporated. Pour the batter into the cake pan and spread it out across the bottom in an even layer.

3. Prepare the topping: Using the same bowl without rinsing, combine the cheese, flour, 2 tablespoons sugar, and lemon zest; beat until smooth. Add the egg yolk and blend in completely. Pour this on top of the batter and spread out evenly, leaving a generous 1-inch border all the way around the edge of the pan.

4. Toss the cherries with the remaining 2 tablespoons sugar, the almond extract, and the cinnamon. Dot the top of the cheese evenly with the cherries and sprinkle on the juices.

5. Bake for 30 to 35 minutes, until the cheese filling is light golden and firm when you shake the pan gently. Let cool in the pan for about 15 minutes before cutting.

DATE AND WALNUT TEA CAKES

MAKES 6 MINI BUNDT CAKES; SERVES 6

Black walnut trees grow all over Nashville. They are not native to the area, but they thrive here, and the nuts are a popular addition to baked goods. We use them whenever possible, but you can make this recipe with either black walnuts or the ordinary kind, which are much easier to find.

1 cup walnut pieces

1½ sticks (6 ounces) unsalted butter, softened

1 cup sugar

½ cup honey

Grated zest of 1 orange

½ teaspoon salt

2 eggs

3 cups unbleached all-purpose flour

1½ teaspoons baking soda

1 cup chopped dates

⅔ cup sour cream

1. Preheat the oven to 350°F. Grease and flour 6 mini ¾-cup Bundt pans. Place the walnuts in a baking dish and toast in the oven until fragrant, 5 to 7 minutes.

2. In a large mixing bowl, combine the butter, sugar, honey, orange zest, and salt. Cream together with an electric mixer on medium speed until light and fluffy, about 3 minutes. Add the eggs, one at a time, and continue beating until fluffy, about 2 minutes longer. Scrape down the bowl.

3. Sift the flour and baking soda over the egg mixture. Fold in by hand a few times. Add the toasted walnuts, dates, and sour cream and continue folding until the batter is evenly mixed with no white streaks. Divide the batter among the mini Bundt pans.

4. Bake for 25 to 30 minutes, until a toothpick or cake tester inserted in the center comes out clean. Let the cakes cool in the pans for about 10 minutes; then turn them out onto a wire rack to cool completely.

PEAR COFFEE CAKE

MAKES A 10-INCH COFFEE CAKE; SERVES 8

Fall in Nashville is a brief season, with warm spells and then sudden drops in temperature. On the cool days we serve more Yankee ingredients like pears and walnuts, though in truth, both flourish in Tennessee. This is a breakfast coffee cake that folks pair with coffee all afternoon.

2 to 3 large pears, such as Anjou

1 cup canola or other neutral vegetable oil

1½ cups sugar

2 eggs

2 cups unbleached all-purpose flour

1 teaspoon baking soda

2 teaspoons ground cinnamon

1 teaspoon ground ginger

¼ cup chopped walnuts

¼ cup packed dark brown sugar

1 Preheat the oven to 350°F. Grease and flour a 10-inch round cake pan. Peel and core the pears and cut them into ½-inch dice; measure out 1½ cups for this recipe.

2 Place the oil, sugar, and eggs in a mixing bowl and whisk until smooth. Sift the flour, baking soda, 1½ teaspoons of the cinnamon, and the ginger over the egg mixture. Fold a few times by hand with a rubber spatula. Toss the pears evenly over the mixture and fold together to mix evenly. Scrape the batter into the prepared pan.

3 In a small bowl, rub the walnuts, brown sugar, and remaining ½ teaspoon cinnamon together until evenly mixed. Sprinkle over the top of the cake batter.

4 Bake for 55 to 60 minutes, until a toothpick or cake tester inserted in the center comes out clean. Let cool in the pan for 15 minutes. Carefully invert the cake onto a plate to unmold; place a small wire rack on top of the cake and invert again right side up. Let the cake cool for about another 15 minutes. Serve warm or at room temperature.

LEMON TUNNEL-OF-LOVE TEA CAKE

MAKE AN 8-INCH BUNDT CAKE; SERVES 8

This is an unusual recipe because it includes only one egg, which does not go into the cake but into the cheesecake ribbon that becomes the "tunnel of love." At the Loveless, we're fans of any dessert that contains the word *love* in the title.

6 ounces cream cheese (*not* reduced-fat or whipped), softened

1⅓ cups plus ¼ cup granulated sugar

½ teaspoon vanilla extract

1 egg

2¼ cups unbleached all-purpose flour

1½ teaspoons baking soda

¼ teaspoon salt

½ cup canola or other neutral vegetable oil

1 tablespoon grated lemon zest

1¼ cups buttermilk

2 tablespoons freshly squeezed lemon juice

1 cup confectioners' sugar

1 Preheat the oven to 350°F. Grease and flour a 6- to 8-cup Bundt pan and set aside.

2 Blend the cream cheese with ¼ cup of the granulated sugar and the vanilla. Scrape the bowl, add the egg, and mix well. Set aside while you prepare the cake batter.

3 Sift the flour, remaining 1⅓ cups granulated sugar, baking soda, and salt into a mixing bowl; whisk briefly to blend. Whisk in the oil, lemon zest, and about half of the buttermilk until smooth. This first addition will prevent lumps from forming, so do not be tempted to pour in all of the liquid at once. Whisk in the remaining buttermilk, mixing only long enough to combine. Pour half of the cake batter into the prepared Bundt pan. Dollop the cream cheese mixture over the batter, trying to center it in the pan so that it doesn't reach either edge. Cover with the remaining batter.

4 Bake for about 55 minutes, until the top is golden brown and slightly firm to the touch. If you check it with a toothpick or cake tester, there should be only traces of cream cheese and no loose batter. Let the cake cool in the pan for 15 minutes, then invert onto a rack to cool completely.

5 To add the final touch, stir the lemon juice into the confectioners' sugar until smooth. Drizzle the glaze over the cake in a random pattern.

UPSIDE-DOWN PECAN PERSIMMON COFFEE CAKE

MAKES A 10-INCH COFFEE CAKE; SERVES 8

This is a decadent treat that makes the search for persimmons worthwhile. Keep in mind that Southern persimmons are very small and seedy, which is why the puree should be made in a food mill rather than a food processor. If you don't have persimmon trees nearby, substitute the Japanese Hachiya variety.

1 stick (4 ounces) plus 3 tablespoons unsalted butter, softened

1/3 cup honey

1/4 cup granulated sugar

3/4 teaspoon ground cinnamon

1 1/2 cups pecan pieces

1 1/3 cups packed brown sugar

1 teaspoon vanilla extract

1/4 teaspoon salt

2 eggs

2/3 cup persimmon puree (12 to 14 Southern or 2 Hachiya persimmons; see page 27)

2 cups unbleached all-purpose flour

2 1/2 teaspoons baking powder

2/3 cup buttermilk

1 Preheat the oven to 350°F. Grease a 10-inch round cake pan.

2 In a small heavy saucepan, combine 5 tablespoons of the butter, the honey, granulated sugar, and cinnamon. Warm over low heat, stirring to dissolve the sugar. Raise the heat to medium and bring to a boil. Boil for 1 minute, then pour the syrup into the prepared cake pan, tilting to cover the bottom evenly. Scatter the pecans over the bottom of the pan, leaving a 1/2-inch border around the edge.

3 In a mixing bowl, cream the remaining 6 tablespoons butter with the brown sugar, vanilla, and salt until light and fluffy. Beat in the eggs, one at a time, and scrape the bowl well. Add the persimmon puree and combine thoroughly. Sift the flour and baking powder over the batter and fold them in a few times. Sprinkle the buttermilk over the batter and fold until mixed completely. Scrape the batter into the pan carefully, spreading it out gently to avoid disturbing the pecans.

4 Bake for 45 minutes, or until a toothpick or cake tester inserted in the center comes out clean. Let the cake cool in the pan for 5 to 10 minutes. Place a deep round platter over the cake and quickly invert to unmold the cake with the syrup on top; be careful because the syrup will be very hot. Let cool for 10 to 15 minutes; serve warm.

SPICED PUMPKIN-CHOCOLATE CHIP TEA CAKE

MAKES A LARGE BUNDT CAKE; SERVES 12

When the weather turns, and pumpkin pies go on the menu, we always end up with extra pumpkin puree, which is perfect for this moist tea cake. At the cafe it's popular sold by the slice to go.

2⅓ cups packed dark brown sugar

1½ cups canola or other neutral vegetable oil

1 cup canned pumpkin puree

3 eggs

3 cups unbleached all-purpose flour

1 teaspoon baking soda

2¼ teaspoons ground cinnamon

1 teaspoon ground ginger

½ teaspoon ground cardamom

¼ teaspoon ground cloves

½ cup chocolate chips

⅓ cup chopped walnut pieces

Confectioners' sugar (optional)

1. Preheat the oven to 350°F. Grease and flour a 10- to 12-cup Bundt pan.

2. Place 2 cups of the brown sugar in a large mixing bowl and break it up to remove any lumps. Add the oil, pumpkin puree, and eggs. Whisk together until smooth. Sift the flour, baking soda, 2 teaspoons of the cinnamon, the ginger, cardamom, and cloves over the pumpkin mixture. Add the chocolate chips and fold until the batter is evenly mixed and no streaks remain.

3. In a small bowl, combine the remaining ⅓ cup brown sugar and remaining ¼ teaspoon cinnamon with the walnuts. Rub together with your fingertips until well blended. Pour half of the pumpkin batter into the prepared Bundt pan. Sprinkle the walnut mixture over the top of the batter, trying to keep it in the center. Cover with the remaining batter.

4. Bake for 60 to 70 minutes, until a toothpick or cake tester inserted in the center comes out clean. Let the cake cool in the pan for about 10 minutes. Then turn out onto a rack to cool completely. Sprinkle with confectioners' sugar, if desired.

Photograph on page 83.

TIPSY CAKE

MAKES 3 SMALL LOAVES; SERVES 4 TO 6 EACH

We used to carry two kinds of tipsy cakes made by a popular local bakery that drowned its desserts in liberal amounts of a famous Tennessee whiskey (which will not be named here). Unfortunately, when the booze producer raised its prices too high, the bakery closed. To fill the void, we developed our own recipe made with bourbon.

1¼ cups golden raisins

½ cup plus 6 tablespoons bourbon

1 stick (4 ounces) unsalted butter, softened

1 cup packed light brown sugar

¼ teaspoon salt

3 eggs

1¼ cups unbleached all-purpose flour

¾ teaspoon baking soda

¼ teaspoon freshly grated nutmeg

¾ cup pecan pieces

1. Preheat the oven to 325°F. Grease and flour 3 loaf pans, 5 by 3 by 2 inches.

2. In a small saucepan, bring the golden raisins and ½ cup of the bourbon to a boil over medium-low heat. Immediately remove from the heat and let the raisins steep until cooled completely.

3. In a mixing bowl, cream the butter, brown sugar, and salt together with an electric mixer on medium speed until light and fluffy. Add the eggs, one at a time, scraping the bowl before each addition. Sift the flour, baking soda, and nutmeg over the batter and fold a few times. Add the raisins with any bourbon not absorbed and the pecan pieces. Fold the batter together thoroughly. Divide evenly among the pans.

4. Bake for 40 minutes, or until a toothpick or cake tester inserted in the center of a cake comes out clean. Let the cakes cool in the pans for 10 minutes. Then turn them out onto a rack and brush each one with 2 tablespoons of the remaining bourbon. Let cool completely before slicing.

VARIATION: CHOCOLATE TIPSY CAKE

Prepare the recipe for Tipsy Cake as directed, substituting 1¼ cups granulated sugar for the brown sugar, reducing the flour to 1 cup, adding ⅓ cup unsweetened cocoa powder (*not* Dutch process) with the flour, omitting the nutmeg, and baking the cake for 45 to 50 minutes.

Tipsy Cake (left) and Chocolate Tipsy Cake (right)

BANANA SPLIT CHEESECAKE

MAKES AN 8-INCH CHEESECAKE; SERVES 10

Every now and then we have an abundance of overripe bananas that are not suitable for much besides baking. Combine that with our usual supply of chocolate, cream cheese, and fresh strawberries and you get this: a banana cheesecake marbled with chocolate in a cookie crust. Along with fresh strawberry sauce, you could easily add some banana slices, pineapple chunks, and a scoop of whipped cream.

1½ cups cookie crumbs, made from Chocolate Wafers (page 174), store-bought vanilla or chocolate wafers, or graham crackers

⅔ cup plus 6 tablespoons sugar

5 tablespoons unsalted butter, melted and still hot

1 pound cream cheese (*not* reduced-fat or whipped)

½ cup mashed very ripe banana (1 to 2 bananas)

¼ cup sour cream

2 tablespoons unbleached all-purpose flour

4 eggs

1 ounce unsweetened chocolate, melted (see page 36)

2 cups fresh strawberries

Whipped cream and chopped walnuts for garnish

1. Preheat the oven to 300°F. Grease an 8-inch round heavy aluminum pan.

2. In a small bowl, combine the cookie crumbs and 3 tablespoons of the sugar. Stir to mix well. Pour in the melted butter and toss together to moisten evenly. Dump the crumb mixture into the prepared pan and press to cover the bottom and three-quarters of the way up the sides.

3. To make the filling, place the cream cheese, ⅔ cup of the remaining sugar, the banana, sour cream, and flour in a food processor; pulse to form a smooth paste. With the machine on, add the eggs, one at a time; scrape down the bowl and pulse briefly.

4. Measure out 1¼ cups of the cream cheese filling and set it aside. Scrape the remaining filling into the prepared pan. Return 1 cup of the reserved filling to the food processor. Add the melted chocolate and combine, scraping the sides of the bowl well to make sure the batter is evenly mixed. Drizzle the chocolate filling in an abstract ribbon pattern over the top of the cream cheese filling in the pan. Drizzle the remaining ¼ cup banana filling over the chocolate and use a blunt knife or bamboo skewer to swirl them into a marbled pattern; do not overmix.

continued

5 Bake in the center of the oven for 45 minutes. Remove the cake from the oven and run a knife all the way around the edges to release the cake and crust. Return the cheesecake to the oven, turn off the heat, and let stand without opening the door for 15 minutes. Remove the cake from the oven and let stand in the pan on a rack until cooled to room temperature. Cover and refrigerate the cake for at least 3 hours, or preferably overnight, to set completely.

6 To remove the cake from the pan, wrap a flat plate or tray with plastic wrap and spray it lightly with nonstick cooking spray. Hold the bottom of the cake pan over low heat until it is slightly warm but not hot. Gently shake the pan from side to side to release the cheesecake. Place the greased plate over the top of the cake and quickly invert it. The cake should slide right out of the pan. Place your serving plate on the bottom of the cake and invert it again right side up.

7 To make the strawberry sauce, place the strawberries and remaining 3 tablespoons sugar in a blender or food processor and puree until smooth.

8 To cut the cake, use a large chef's knife dipped in hot water and wiped clean between cuts. Serve each slice with a drizzle of strawberry sauce. Top with a garnish of whipped cream and chopped walnuts.

The Secret of Loveless's Perfect Cheesecake

For a rich and creamy cheesecake that does not crack, always follow these rules:

1. Throw away your springform pans and use a heavy-gauge round aluminum cake pan instead.

2. Never mind using a water bath; it's a dangerous waste of time.

3. Make sure you use a plain, nonwhipped, full-fat cream cheese for your cheesecakes.

4. Always use a food processor rather than an electric mixer to blend the cheesecake filling because it will not incorporate unwanted air.

5. Immediately after baking, be sure to release the cake by running a knife around it, or the top will crack like a canyon. Then return it to the hot, turned-off oven to finish cooking.

6. Testing for doneness is tricky but not necessary if you follow the recipe exactly. However, if you must, the cake should feel firm around the edges and slightly firm in the center. Do not insert a knife, or you will give the cake a place to crack.

7. You'll notice that these cheesecake recipes contain just a little bit of flour. This helps bind the ingredients, but the baked filling will be smooth and creamy.

KEY LIME–WHITE CHOCOLATE CHEESECAKE

MAKES AN 8-INCH CHEESECAKE; SERVES 10

Classic Southern Key lime pie gets a Nashville spin here, as it's morphed into a tangy cheesecake topped with white chocolate whipped cream, an irresistible combination that is very popular at the cafe. For the crust, we use crumbs from plain biscotti. You can follow suit or substitute graham crackers or gingersnaps.

1½ cups cookie crumbs, made from plain biscotti, gingersnaps, graham crackers, or a combination of gingersnaps and graham crackers

⅔ cup plus 3 tablespoons sugar

5 tablespoons unsalted butter, melted and still hot

1 pound cream cheese (*not* reduced-fat or whipped)

⅓ cup sour cream

2 tablespoons unbleached all-purpose flour

1½ teaspoons grated lime zest

4 eggs

⅓ cup fresh or bottled Key lime juice

2 ounces pure white chocolate, chopped

⅔ cup heavy cream

White chocolate shavings for garnish

1. Preheat the oven to 300°F. Grease an 8-inch round heavy aluminum cake pan.

2. In a small bowl, combine the cookie crumbs with 3 tablespoons of the sugar and mix well. Pour in the melted butter and toss to moisten evenly. Dump the crumb mixture into the cake pan and press evenly over the bottom and three-quarters of the way up the sides.

3. To make the filling, place the cream cheese, remaining ⅔ cup sugar, sour cream, flour, and lime zest in a food processor and pulse to form a smooth paste. With the machine on, add the eggs through the feed tube, one at a time; scrape down the sides of the bowl. Add the Key lime juice and process to blend. Scrape the filling into the prepared pan.

4. Bake in the center of the oven for 45 minutes. Remove the cake from the oven and run a knife all the way around the edges to release the cake. Return the cheesecake to the oven, turn off the heat, and let stand without opening the door for another 15 minutes. Remove the cake from the oven and let cool completely. Cover the cheesecake and refrigerate for at least 3 hours, preferably overnight.

5 To remove the cake from the pan, wrap a flat plate or tray with plastic wrap and spray it lightly with nonstick cooking spray. Hold the bottom of the cake pan over low heat until it is slightly warm but not hot. Gently shake the pan from side to side to release the cake. Place the greased plate over the top of the cake and invert it. The cheesecake should slide right out of the pan. Place your serving plate on the bottom of the cake and invert it again so that it is right side up.

6 To make the white chocolate whipped cream, melt the white chocolate with 2 tablespoons of the heavy cream in a small, heavy saucepan. Remove from the heat and let cool to body temperature. With an electric mixer, whip the remaining cream to soft peaks. Add the melted white chocolate and mix well. Whip the white chocolate cream until slightly stiffer peaks form. It will not be as stiff as plain whipped cream; do not overbeat, or the cream and white chocolate may separate. Spread the topping over the cake and refrigerate for at least 1 hour, until set. Sprinkle with the white chocolate shavings. To cut the cake, use a large chef's knife dipped in hot water and wiped clean between cuts to yield perfectly smooth slices of cake.

TURTLE CHEESECAKE

MAKES AN 8-INCH CHEESECAKE; SERVES 10

Turtle Pie (page 37) is a favorite at the cafe, where anything sweet gets four stars. The combination of caramel, pecans, and chocolate also makes for a great cheesecake. The caramel goes directly into the cheesecake filling, and the chocolate and pecans form a candylike topping.

1½ cups cookie crumbs, made from plain biscotti or graham crackers

3 tablespoons granulated sugar

5 tablespoons unsalted butter, melted

1 pound cream cheese (*not* reduced-fat or whipped)

½ cup prepared caramel, such as Mexican *cajeta* or *dulce de leche* (see Sources, page 210)

½ cup packed dark brown sugar

⅓ cup sour cream

2 tablespoons unbleached all-purpose flour

1 teaspoon vanilla extract

4 eggs

4 ounces semisweet chocolate, chopped

⅓ cup half-and-half

⅓ cup pecan pieces

1. Preheat the oven to 300°F. Grease an 8-inch round heavy aluminum cake pan.

2. In a small bowl, combine the cookie crumbs and granulated sugar and mix well. Pour in the melted butter and toss to moisten evenly. Dump the crumb mixture into the prepared pan and press evenly over the bottom and about three-quarters of the way up the sides.

3. To make the cheesecake filling, place the cream cheese, caramel, brown sugar, sour cream, flour, and vanilla in a food processor and pulse to form a smooth paste. With the machine on, add the eggs through the feed tube, one at a time; scrape the sides of the bowl and pulse briefly to make sure the batter is mixed evenly. Scrape the filling into the prepared pan.

4. Bake in the center of the oven for 45 minutes. Remove the cake from the oven and run a knife all the way around the edges to release the cake from the pan. Return the cheesecake to the oven, turn off the heat, and let the cake stand without opening the door for another 20 minutes. Remove the cake from the oven and let cool completely. Cover and refrigerate until set, at least 3 hours, or preferably overnight.

5 To remove the cake from the pan, wrap a flat plate or tray with plastic wrap and spray it lightly with nonstick cooking spray. Hold the bottom of the cake pan over low heat until it is slightly warm but not hot. Gently shake the pan from side to side to release the cake. Place the greased plate over the top of the cake and invert it. The cake should slide right out of the pan. Place your serving plate on the bottom of the cake and invert it again right side up.

6 To make the chocolate-pecan topping, melt the chocolate and half-and-half in a pan set over (not in) barely simmering water, whisking until smooth. Spread the chocolate cream over the cold cake and sprinkle the pecans on top. Let set in the refrigerator for at least 1 hour. To cut the cake, use a large chef's knife dipped in hot water and wiped clean between cuts to yield perfectly smooth slices of cake.

Cookies, Bars, and Cupcakes

Peanut Butter–Chocolate Chip Granola Cookies (page 168)

What can't a good cookie do? It staves off hunger, it's perfectly portable, and, crumbs be damned, you can even sneak one or two into your pocket. Put out a plate of cookies in any room, and it will demonstrate a gravitational pull that rivals celestial bodies.

Sure, cookies are about the most casual and easy dessert imaginable, but we take great pride in them at the Loveless Cafe. Why? Because cookies are the most reliable and flexible desserts we know, good for any occasion. We do them right, baked up in endless variations with the best ingredients we can get our hands on. We start with sweet butter and then look to local growers for our honey, sorghum, and pecans, building a rich foundation for many of the recipes.

What makes cookies so popular is that there truly is one for everyone—with such a breadth of texture and flavor that aficionados of chewy texture can sit at the same table with those who prefer a crispy crunch. Do you like fruit and nuts? Go crazy with Chocolate Cherry Cha-chas. Are you a minimalist? Seek solace in the purity of the best sugar cookie you will ever find

with our Sugar Bowl Cookies.
Need to reward the kids?
Our Peanut Butter-Chocolate
Chip Granola Cookies are a
satisfying treat.

A few of the bar cookies, like our Southern Pecan Squares
and Lady Lemon Bars, may sound a bit more complicated at
first, but we've come up with a simple pat-in-the-pan crust that
anyone can master. Like our bars, Loveless cupcakes are deceptive
in size but brim with incredible richness. The addition of fresh
fruit in the Strawberry Cupcakes and fresh vegetables in the
Victory Garden Cupcakes adds to their remarkable flavor.

Cookies can be saviors on those busiest of days. They can
soothe an empty stomach and help make anticipation of your
next meal all the sweeter. With the instant gratification of a
cookie in hand, time just seems to pass a little more quickly,
especially when that time involves waiting to get a table at the
Loveless Cafe.

CHOCOLATE CHERRY CHA-CHAS

MAKES ABOUT 4 DOZEN COOKIES

On those rare occasions when things are slow in the cafe, we play around with new recipes. If something works out well and makes it onto the menu, we look for a catchy, enticing name that reflects the dessert and our lively Loveless personality. We tossed around dozens of ideas for these chewy chocolate cookies loaded with dried cherries, raisins, and chocolate chips until someone yelled out, "Cha-chas!" and the name stuck.

1²/₃ cups unbleached all-purpose flour

²/₃ cup unsweetened cocoa powder

1 teaspoon baking soda

2 sticks (8 ounces) unsalted butter, softened

1¹/₃ cups packed light brown sugar

1 teaspoon vanilla extract

½ teaspoon salt

2 eggs

¾ cup semisweet chocolate chips

¾ cup dried cherries

¾ cup raisins

1. Preheat the oven to 375°F. Line 2 sturdy cookie sheets with parchment paper or silicone liners.

2. Sift the flour, cocoa, and baking soda into a bowl and set aside. In a mixing bowl, cream the butter, brown sugar, vanilla, and salt with an electric mixer on medium speed until light and fluffy. Beat in the eggs, one at a time, and scrape the bowl well. Add the dry ingredients and mix just until no streaks remain.

3. Fold in the chocolate chips, dried cherries, and raisins by hand. Drop the dough by heaping tablespoons at least 2 inches apart onto the prepared baking sheets.

4. Bake for 14 minutes, rotating the pans halfway through the baking time. Remove the cookies from the oven while they still look a little underdone; they will crisp up when they set. Let cool on the pans for a few minutes to firm up slightly, then transfer to a wire rack to cool completely.

COCONUT CHEWS

MAKES ABOUT 3½ DOZEN COOKIES

When Paula Deen visited the restaurant, she was absolutely clear about her yen for coconut. These rich, buttery cookies loaded with coconut were her hands-down favorites. She even packed up a few strays that were left on the plate and took them with her.

2 sticks (8 ounces) unsalted butter, softened

1½ cups sugar

1 teaspoon vanilla extract

2 eggs

2⅓ cups unbleached all-purpose flour

1 teaspoon baking soda

1 pound sweetened shredded coconut

1 Preheat the oven to 375°F. Line 2 sturdy cookie sheets with parchment paper or silicone liners.

2 In a mixing bowl, cream the butter, sugar, and vanilla with an electric mixer on medium speed until light and fluffy. Beat in the eggs, one at a time, and scrape the bowl. Add the flour and baking soda and mix until combined.

3 Fold in the coconut by hand. Drop the dough by heaping tablespoons about 2 inches apart onto the prepared cookie sheets.

4 Bake for 15 minutes, rotating the pans halfway through the baking time. The cookies are done when they spread out and turn golden around the edges. Let cool completely before serving, if you can wait that long.

OATMEAL COOKIES WITH DRIED PEACHES

MAKES ABOUT 2½ DOZEN COOKIES

It was the dried peaches we always toss into the granola we make at the Loveless that inspired these oatmeal cookies. No one can identify the secret ingredient—the peaches—which is now your secret too.

1¼ cups unbleached all-purpose flour

1⅓ cups rolled oats

1 teaspoon baking soda

½ teaspoon ground cinnamon

1 stick (4 ounces) unsalted butter, softened

1 cup sugar

2 tablespoons sorghum or molasses

1 teaspoon vanilla extract

1 egg

3 ounces dried peaches, cut into ¼-inch dice

1. Preheat the oven to 350°F. Line 2 sturdy cookie sheets with parchment paper or silicone liners.

2. In a medium bowl, combine the flour, oats, baking soda, and cinnamon and stir to combine. In a mixing bowl, cream the butter, sugar, sorghum, and vanilla with an electric mixer on medium speed until light and fluffy. Beat in the egg and scrape the sides of the bowl. Add the flour mixture and blend until just barely combined; some streaks of flour should still show.

3. Sprinkle the dried peaches over the dough and fold in by hand until evenly mixed with no streaks remaining. Drop the dough by heaping tablespoons about 2 inches apart onto the prepared cookie sheets.

4. Bake for 16 minutes, rotating the pans halfway through the baking time. Let the cookies set for a few minutes, then transfer to wire racks to cool completely.

PEANUT BUTTER–CHOCOLATE CHIP GRANOLA COOKIES

MAKES ABOUT 3 DOZEN COOKIES

At the cafe, our homemade granola is loaded with pecans, honey, and sorghum. Even though these great snacking cookies are not exactly health food, they do contain more protein and fiber than most.

1 stick (4 ounces) unsalted butter, softened

½ cup peanut butter

¾ cup packed dark brown sugar

1 egg

1 cup unbleached all-purpose flour

½ teaspoon baking soda

2 cups granola (Loveless Homemade Granola—see Sources, page 210—or your favorite brand)

⅔ cup semisweet chocolate chips

1. Preheat the oven to 350°F. Line 2 sturdy cookie sheets with parchment paper or silicone liners.

2. In a mixing bowl, cream the butter and peanut butter with an electric mixer on medium speed until combined. Scrape the sides of the bowl and the beaters and add the brown sugar. Beat until light and fluffy, about 3 minutes. Add the egg and mix to combine.

3. By hand, fold in the flour and baking soda a few times. Add the granola and chocolate chips and fold until the dough is well mixed. Drop the dough by heaping tablespoons about 2 inches apart onto the prepared cookie sheets.

4. Bake for 15 minutes, turning the pans and rotating from top to bottom halfway through the baking time. The cookies should have a slightly golden edge and appear a little fluffy and soft. Baking them longer will result in crispy-crunchy cookies rather than soft, chewy ones. Let the cookies set for a few minutes; then transfer to a rack to cool completely.

Baking Tips

• Be sure to use a peanut butter that has been homogenized. Whether it is chunky or smooth is up to you.

• If you don't make your own granola and you want cookies the same consistency as those we serve in the cafe, choose a brand that is relatively low in fat and has no added fruit.

SUGAR BOWL COOKIES

MAKES ABOUT 2 DOZEN 3-INCH COOKIES

These are simply the best sugar cookies in Nashville, or so says the crew here. Rolled thin and baked to a crisp, these are truly irresistible, especially when you let them get a tad darker than usual so the sugar caramelizes throughout the cookie. Because they are so simple, you can change the shape and color to reflect the seasons and holidays.

1¾ sticks (7 ounces) unsalted butter, softened

1 cup granulated sugar

1 teaspoon vanilla extract

¼ teaspoon salt

1 egg

2½ cups unbleached all-purpose flour, plus more for rolling the dough

Colored coarse sugar

1 Preheat the oven to 350°F. Line 2 sturdy cookie sheets with parchment paper or silicone liners.

2 In a mixing bowl, cream the butter, granulated sugar, vanilla, and salt with an electric mixer on medium speed until light and fluffy. Add the egg and beat until blended; scrape down the sides of the bowl. Add the flour and fold by hand until the mixture comes together to form a smooth dough. Scrape the dough out of the bowl and form it into a thick patty; wrap in plastic and refrigerate for at least 1 hour or as long as 3 days before rolling it out.

3 On a floured board, roll out the dough about ⅜ inch thick. Using a 3-inch cutter, cut into rounds, or choose another shape if you prefer. Gather up the scraps and roll out one more time; cut into more rounds. Sprinkle the cookies liberally with colored sugar.

4 Bake for 16 to 18 minutes, until the cookies are golden brown around the edges. Let set on the sheets for 5 minutes; then transfer to a wire rack to cool completely.

Baking Tip: See "A Foolproof Method for Rolling Out Cookie Dough" on pages 172–73.

SNICKERDOODLES

MAKES ABOUT 3 DOZEN COOKIES

These are classic cinnamon–sugar cookies, which we've lightened and made richer at the same time by replacing some of the butter with cream cheese. Sometimes on Wednesdays, when Music City Roots broadcasts live from the Loveless Barn, we bake these monster size and send them up to the food concession, where they often disappear even before the musicians are finished tuning up.

1 stick (4 ounces) unsalted butter, softened

4 ounces cream cheese (*not* reduced-fat or whipped), softened

2½ cups sugar

1 teaspoon vanilla extract

2 eggs

3 cups unbleached all-purpose flour

½ teaspoon baking soda

½ teaspoon cream of tartar

2 teaspoons ground cinnamon

1. Preheat the oven to 375°F. Line 2 sturdy cookie sheets with parchment paper or silicone liners.

2. Cream the butter, cream cheese, 1¾ cups of the sugar, and the vanilla with an electric mixer on medium speed until light and fluffy. Add the eggs, one at a time, and scrape the sides of the bowl. Sift the flour, baking soda, and cream of tartar over the mixture and fold together by hand until no streaks remain.

3. In a wide bowl, mix the remaining ¾ cup sugar with the cinnamon. Scoop out a heaping tablespoon of the dough and roll it into a ball. Roll the ball in the cinnamon sugar to coat and set on the lined cookie sheets. Repeat to use all the dough, setting the cookies about 2 inches apart.

4. Bake for about 14 minutes, until the cookies are set around the edges and lightly browned on the bottom but still slightly soft in the middle. Transfer to racks to cool. They'll firm up as they set.

A Foolproof Method for Rolling Out Cookie Dough

A couple of easy tricks can turn rough homemade cookies into polished professional-looking confections. The only special equipment you need is a couple of thin wooden dowels, available in baking and craft shops, and a soft bristle brush. You can use this technique with Sugar Bowl Cookies (page 170) and Chocolate Wafers (page 174) or for any rolled cookie dough.

EQUIPMENT NEEDED

- large rolling pin
- large, flat rolling surface
- mesh strainer or sifter
- long ⅜-inch wooden dowels
- soft 2-inch natural-bristle brush

1. Allow your refrigerated cookie dough to soften slightly until pliable but not sticky. Break off a piece that is the equivalent of about 2 cups of dough. Knead the dough a few times on a lightly floured surface to make it smooth and easy to work with. Shape it into a rectangle.

2. Give yourself plenty of room on a clean, level countertop or table. Using a mesh strainer or sifter, liberally coat the rolling surface with flour. Lay the dowels down on the work surface so that they are parallel to each other with 10 to 12 inches in between them—the same width as the rolling pin.

3. Place the dough between the dowels and generously sprinkle it with flour. Begin rolling the dough, using strokes that go toward and away from your body.

4. After several strokes, carefully lift the dough and give it a quarter turn. Be sure to keep the surfaces of the dough floured to prevent sticking. Keep rolling, lifting and flouring the dough as you go, until it is the same thickness as the dowels.

5. Use the brush to clear all the flour from the top of the dough.

6. Cut the dough into whatever cookie shape you desire.

7. Carefully turn each cookie over onto a clean workspace and brush off the excess flour before placing on the cookie sheet and baking as directed.

To rework the scraps, brush off as much excess flour as possible, gently knead them together, and repeat the rolling process. After you have cut out more cookies, you may be able to repeat this process one more time, but the third batch will be drier and more crumbly; the flavor may even be muted. The toughness of the dough will depend on how much extra flour is worked in during the process, so you want to brush off as much as possible. If at any time the dough becomes soft and sticky, chill it until it firms up again.

Why go to this extreme? Consistency. If all of the cookies are a different thickness, some will be underdone while others will burn on the same tray. With this technique, your cookies will look as perfect as a professional pastry chef's.

CHOCOLATE WAFERS

MAKES ABOUT 20 WAFERS

It's true; chocolate wafer cookies are easy to buy, but what a difference in taste and texture with homemade. For perfect, professional-looking cookies, follow the instructions for rolling out cookie dough (pages 172–73).

1 cup unbleached all-purpose flour

2/3 cup confectioners' sugar

1/4 cup plus 2 tablespoons unsweetened cocoa powder

1/4 teaspoon ground cinnamon

1 stick (4 ounces) cold unsalted butter, cut into cubes

1 teaspoon vanilla extract

Coarse sugar

1. Preheat the oven to 350°F. Line 2 baking sheets with parchment paper or silicone liners.

2. Place the flour, confectioners' sugar, cocoa powder, and cinnamon in the bowl of a food processor and pulse to blend. Sprinkle the butter cubes over the mixture and pulse to cut it in. Add the vanilla and process just until a smooth dough forms.

3. Remove the dough from the machine and form into 2 thick disks. On a lightly floured surface, roll out each disk about 3/8 inch thick. Using a 2 3/4-inch round cutter, cut out at least 18 circles. Rework the scraps once or twice and roll out a couple extra. Place the wafers about 1 inch apart on the prepared pans. Prick them a few times with a fork and sprinkle the tops with coarse sugar.

4. Bake for about 12 minutes, rotating the pans after 6 minutes, until crisp. Let set on the sheet for 5 to 10 minutes, then transfer to a wire rack to cool completely before using.

Baking Tip: These wafers can be baked as long as 4 days ahead, but they need to be stored in an airtight tin to retain their crisp, flaky texture.

ONE-BOWL BROWNIE DROPS

MAKES ABOUT 2½ DOZEN COOKIES

These fudgy cookies will stay soft for up to three days in an airtight tin.

¾ cup chopped walnuts

4 ounces unsweetened chocolate, chopped

5 tablespoons unsalted butter

1⅓ cups sugar

2 eggs

1 teaspoon vanilla extract

⅓ cup unbleached all-purpose flour

½ teaspoon baking powder

¾ cup semisweet chocolate chips

1. Preheat the oven to 350°F. Line 2 sturdy cookie sheets with parchment paper or silicone liners.

2. Toast the walnuts in a baking dish for 5 to 7 minutes, until lightly browned and fragrant. Transfer to a plate and let cool.

3. Place the chocolate and butter in a heatproof bowl set over (not in) a pan of barely simmering water. Heat, stirring often, until the chocolate melts, 3 to 5 minutes. Remove from the heat.

4. Add the sugar, eggs, and vanilla to the melted chocolate and butter. With an electric mixer on medium speed, beat until well blended. Sift the flour and baking powder over the batter and fold in by hand. Add the walnuts and chocolate chips, stirring just enough to combine. Drop the dough by tablespoons at least 2 inches apart onto the lined cookie sheets.

5. Bake for exactly 12 minutes. Remove from the oven and let stand for 2 minutes before carefully transferring the cookies to a wire rack to finish cooling.

BLONDIES

As hard as it is for many of us to believe, not everyone likes chocolate—especially in the South, where lighter flavors seem to shine. With this in mind, we frequently add these bars laced with coconut, pecans, and white chocolate to the tray of goodies for sale on top of the pie showcase in the cafe.

1 stick (4 ounces) plus
2 tablespoons unsalted butter,
softened

1⅓ cups packed light brown
sugar

2 eggs

1⅓ cups unbleached
all-purpose flour

1¼ teaspoons baking powder

½ cup sweetened shredded
coconut

½ cup pecan pieces

½ cup white chocolate chips

1. Preheat the oven to 350°F. Grease a 10-inch square cake pan, line the bottom with parchment paper, and grease the paper.

2. In a mixing bowl, cream the butter and brown sugar with an electric mixer on medium speed until light and fluffy. Add the eggs, one at a time, beating well and scraping down the bowl between additions. Sift the flour and baking powder over the batter and fold a few times. Dump the coconut, pecans, and white chocolate chips over the batter and fold together until no streaks of flour are visible. Scrape the batter into the prepared pan.

3. Bake for 45 minutes, or until a toothpick or cake tester inserted in the center comes out looking almost clean and the surface feels set when touched lightly. Let the blondies cool completely before cutting. To remove them from the pan, briefly warm the bottom of the pan over low heat and invert to unmold onto a cutting board. Carefully peel off the paper, place another cutting board on top, and invert again right side up. Cut into the desired size squares with a large sharp knife.

Baking Tip: To make sure the edges of the blondies do not scorch, use a heavy baking pan.

DOUBLE-CHOCOLATE FUDGE BROWNIES

MAKES SIXTEEN 2-INCH BROWNIES

Intensely chocolate and just a bit fudgy, these brownies can serve many purposes. They're great whenever you crave a little bite of chocolate. And they can be used as a base for other desserts, such as a brownie sundae or the Brownie Bread Pudding on page 208.

1 stick (4 ounces) plus
2 tablespoons unsalted butter

2½ ounces unsweetened
chocolate, chopped

3 eggs

1¼ cups sugar

1 teaspoon finely ground coffee
beans

1 teaspoon vanilla extract

¾ cup plus 2 tablespoons
unbleached all-purpose flour

⅓ cup unsweetened cocoa
powder

½ teaspoon baking powder

½ cup semisweet chocolate
chips

1. Preheat the oven to 350°F. Grease an 8-inch square cake pan, line the bottom with parchment paper, and grease the paper.

2. Place the butter and unsweetened chocolate in a microwave-safe bowl. Using the lowest heat setting or the defrost setting, melt the butter and chocolate in 30-second to 1-minute intervals, stirring until smooth.

3. In a mixing bowl, whisk the eggs with the sugar, ground coffee, and vanilla. Whisk in the chocolate mixture. Sift the flour, cocoa powder, and baking powder over the batter in the bowl. Fold a few times, add ¼ cup of the chocolate chips, and fold until well mixed. Pour the batter into the prepared pan and scatter the remaining ¼ cup chocolate chips evenly over the top.

4. Bake for 30 minutes, until the top feels slightly firm but not at all stiff or hard. Do not wait for the brownies to pull away from the sides of the pan; they will be overbaked at that point. Let the brownies cool completely in the pan. Let the blondies cool completely before cutting. To remove them from the pan, briefly warm the bottom of the pan over low heat and invert to unmold onto a cutting board. Carefully peel off the paper, place another cutting board on top, and invert again right side up. Use a sharp knife to cut into 16 squares.

JESSE'S MAMA'S WICKED BROWNIES

MAKES 25 SMALL OR 16 LARGE BROWNIES

Jesse Goldstein, one of the managers of the Loveless, remembers that every time his grandmother visited she requested a batch of his mama's "wicked brownies." He passed the recipe on to the cafe, where the cakey and chewy brownies, wickedly endowed with walnuts and raisins, convey a little bit of heaven.

3 eggs

2 cups packed dark brown sugar

1 teaspoon almond extract

1 teaspoon vanilla extract

1 stick (4 ounces) unsalted butter, melted and cooled slightly

1 cup self-rising flour

½ cup unsweetened cocoa powder

1½ cups walnut pieces

½ cup semisweet chocolate chips

½ cup raisins

1. Preheat the oven to 350°F. Grease a 10-inch square cake pan, line the bottom with parchment paper, and grease the paper.

2. Place the eggs, brown sugar, almond extract, and vanilla in a bowl. With an electric mixer on medium speed, whip until thick and pale, about 5 minutes. Slowly beat in the melted butter. Sift the flour and cocoa powder over the mixture and fold it in. Fold in the walnuts, chocolate chips, and raisins. Turn the batter into the prepared pan.

3. Bake for about 40 minutes, until the batter rises and sets but is still slightly soft to the touch. Let the brownies cool completely in the pan.

4. To cut the brownies, briefly warm the bottom of the pan over low heat and invert the brownies onto a flat tray. Remove the paper and place a cutting board on top of the brownies. Invert them again right side up and use a large sharp knife to cut them into squares or rectangles.

PEANUT BUTTER BROWNIES

MAKES 24 SMALL OR 12 LARGE BROWNIES

Peanuts are quintessentially Southern. We munch on them roasted, stir them into stews, and smear the butter on waffles and pancakes. So what better pairing for a good ol' country dessert than peanut butter and chocolate?

2 sticks (8 ounces) plus 2 tablespoons unsalted butter

½ cup smooth homogenized peanut butter

2 cups sugar

4 eggs

1 teaspoon vanilla extract

1½ cups unbleached all-purpose flour

1 teaspoon baking powder

4 ounces unsweetened chocolate, chopped

1 teaspoon finely ground coffee beans

3 tablespoons unsweetened cocoa powder (*not* Dutch process)

¼ cup semisweet chocolate chips

1 Preheat the oven to 350°F. Grease a 9 by 13-inch baking pan, line the bottom with parchment paper, and grease the paper.

2 To make the peanut butter batter, place 1 stick plus 2 tablespoons of the butter and the peanut butter in a heatproof bowl set over (not in) a pan of barely simmering water. Warm, stirring, until melted, about 5 minutes. Remove from the heat and whisk in 1 cup of the sugar until blended. Whisk in 2 of the eggs and ½ teaspoon of the vanilla. Sift 1 cup of the flour and the baking powder over the batter and fold in until no streaks remain.

3 To make the chocolate batter, place the remaining 1 stick butter and the unsweetened chocolate in a second heatproof bowl set over (not in) a pan of barely simmering water. Heat, stirring occasionally, until melted, 3 to 5 minutes. Remove from the heat and whisk in the remaining 1 cup sugar, 2 eggs, and ½ teaspoon vanilla as well as the ground coffee. Sift the remaining ½ cup flour and the cocoa powder over the batter; fold until blended. Fold in the chocolate chips.

4 Alternately pour portions of each batter into the prepared pan so that you create a patchwork of batter. Using the handle of a wooden spoon, swirl the two flavors together, taking care to distribute the batter evenly in the pan, filling it to the corners.

5 Bake for 40 minutes. Remove from the oven and let cool completely in the pan. To unmold, briefly warm the bottom of the pan on the stove over low heat. Place a baking sheet over the top of the brownies and invert them quickly so they drop out. Peel off the paper, place another baking sheet or a lightweight cutting board on top, and invert again. Cut into 12 or 24 brownies.

SOUTHERN PECAN SQUARES

MAKES 24 BARS

Like a ripe peach in the middle of summer, fresh pecans in season are much richer and fuller in flavor than commercially processed nuts that have been stored for months. In Tennessee and all across the South, the newly picked nuts are sold in the fall in markets and along the sides of the road. Here at the Loveless, we use this time of year to enjoy them in as many desserts as possible. These nutty bars are classic but heavenly—a pecan pie turned into a bar cookie.

Double recipe Lattice Dough (page 53)

2 sticks (8 ounces) unsalted butter

¾ cup packed light brown sugar

¾ cup honey

¼ cup heavy cream

1 teaspoon vanilla extract

4 cups pecan pieces

½ teaspoon ground cinnamon

1 Preheat the oven to 350°F. Grease a 9 by 13-inch baking pan, line the bottom with parchment paper, and grease the paper.

2 Pat the dough into the prepared baking pan, working it evenly over the bottom and about 1 inch up the sides of the pan. Line the inside of the crust with parchment paper or foil and add enough dried beans or pie weights to reach the top of the crust.

3 Bake for about 20 minutes, until the sides start to brown and the bottom is dry but not colored. Remove from the oven and let cool slightly. Remove the beans and paper.

4 Meanwhile, prepare the filling: Using a heavy 3-quart saucepan, melt the butter with the brown sugar and honey over low heat, stirring occasionally. Raise the heat to medium-low and bring to a slow, rolling boil. Boil for 5 minutes without stirring, but watch carefully. If the syrup begins to boil hard and foams up the side of the pot, reduce the heat, or the caramel will be too hard.

5 Stir in the cream and vanilla and return to a boil for 1 minute; immediately remove from the heat. Stir in the pecans and cinnamon. Pour the hot pecan filling into the crust and place the pan in the oven.

The Perfect Cut

In most of the bar cookie recipes, you'll notice that when it comes time to cut the cookies, we do not suggest simply dividing them up in the pan. For truly professional results, warm the pan briefly over low heat on top of the stove (for which you'll probably want to use oven mitts), and then invert the contents twice: once to unmold the whole dessert onto a tray and then again right side up onto a cutting board. This will allow you to cut the entire block with a large sharp knife into clean, precise rectangles or squares. It also means your baking pans won't get nicked from the knife.

If this seems like too much trouble, of course you can just cut them up in the pan and pry them out with a spatula. To do so, chill them first until set, or they will be too soft too handle. They won't look quite as professional, but they will taste just as good.

6   Bake for 10 to 15 minutes, until bubbly all over. Transfer to a rack and let cool for at least 4 hours or refrigerate overnight. To unmold, gently warm the bottom of the pan over low heat. Place a baking sheet over the top and invert the dessert. Remove the paper. Set a cutting board on top of the unmolded crust and invert again. Cut the bars, now right side up on the board, into 2- or 3-inch squares that can then be cut on the diagonal into smaller triangles.

MAGIC BARS

Biscotti are not on the Loveless menu, but we make them just for the crumbs to use in this yummy confection. This recipe is a version of the classic seven-layer cookie frequently referred to as a "Hello Dolly" in the South. At the cafe they're called Magic Bars because they disappear as fast as we can make them. Be sure to serve them at room temperature.

2 cups cookie crumbs, made from vanilla wafers or biscotti

1 stick (4 ounces) plus 1 tablespoon unsalted butter, melted

1 cup walnut pieces

1 cup sweetened shredded coconut

½ cup semisweet chocolate chips

½ cup white chocolate chips

14-ounce can sweetened condensed milk

1. Preheat the oven to 350°F. Grease an 8-inch square baking dish.

2. In a bowl, toss the cookie crumbs and melted butter together until mixed. Press the mixture evenly over the bottom of the baking dish.

3. Place the walnuts, coconut, semisweet chocolate chips, and white chocolate chips in a bowl and toss to combine. Pour in the sweetened condensed milk and toss again until evenly mixed. Scrape the mixture over the crumb crust in the prepared pan. Moisten your hands lightly and press the mixture into an even layer.

4. Bake for 20 minutes, or until the edges are slightly browned. Remove from the oven and let cool on a rack. When completely set, briefly warm the bottom of the pan over low heat and invert the pastry onto a cutting board. Place a second board on top and quickly invert again right side up. Cut into 2-inch squares with a sharp knife. The bars can be refrigerated for up to a week or frozen for up to a month.

Baking Tips

- If you want to intensify the flavors, toast the coconut and walnuts for 5 to 7 minutes, until lightly browned, and let cool before proceeding with the recipe.

- When baking, be careful not to allow the bars to darken excessively, or they will be dry rather than gooey as they should be.

LADY LEMON BARS

MAKES SIXTEEN 2-INCH BARS

No cookie is more Southern than the lemon bar, with its combination of sweet and tart that comes together in a ladylike confection. Note: The same batter can be baked in mini muffin pans to produce great, bite-sized lemon tartlets (see photo, opposite).

1¼ cups unbleached all-purpose flour

⅓ cup confectioners' sugar, plus additional for sprinkling

6 tablespoons unsalted butter, cut into cubes

1 egg yolk

1 cup granulated sugar

2 whole eggs

1½ teaspoons grated lemon zest

½ cup freshly squeezed lemon juice (about 3 to 4 lemons)

1. Preheat the oven to 350°F. Grease an 8-inch square baking pan, line it with parchment paper, and grease the paper.

2. In a medium bowl, combine 1 cup of the flour with the confectioners' sugar and stir together. Sprinkle the butter cubes over the flour and cut in with 2 knives, a pastry blender, or your fingertips until the mixture resembles coarse meal. Add the egg yolk and work until a soft dough forms. Using your hands, press the dough into the prepared baking pan, spreading it evenly over the bottom and about ½ inch up the sides. Line the crust with parchment paper and fill with dried beans or pie weights.

3. Bake for 20 to 25 minutes, until the dough just begins to color around the edges. Remove from the oven and let cool. Remove the weights and discard the paper.

4. To make the filling, whisk the granulated sugar with the remaining ¼ cup flour in a bowl. Whisk in the whole eggs, lemon zest, and lemon juice. Pour into the crust.

5. Bake for about 25 minutes, until the filling is set. Remove from the oven and run a blunt knife around the edge between the pan and the crust. Let cool slightly, then refrigerate until cooled completely, 1½ to 2 hours.

6. To unmold, line a flat tray with a lightly greased sheet of plastic wrap. Briefly warm the bottom of the pan of bars over low heat. Cover with the lined tray and invert quickly. Carefully peel the paper off the bottom. Place a cutting board on the crust and invert again right side up. Using a sharp knife, cut the lemon bars into the desired size. Sprinkle with additional confectioners' sugar before serving. Refrigerate any leftovers.

Lady Lemon Bars (top), made as tartlets, and Strawberry Jam Bars (bottom, page 188)

STRAWBERRY JAM BARS

MAKES 24 BARS

Carol Fay was our beloved Biscuit Lady here at the Loveless for more than thirty years. Carol loved to cook, but aside from her famous biscuits, she did not do any baking. Once she learned this easy recipe for jam bars by heart, she baked them over and over again for the minister of her church.

1¼ cups unbleached all-purpose flour

1 cup rolled oats

¾ cup packed light brown sugar

1 teaspoon ground cinnamon

¼ teaspoon baking soda

1½ sticks (6 ounces) unsalted butter, cut into cubes

½ cup pecan pieces

1½ cups strawberry preserves

1. Preheat the oven to 350°F. Grease a 9 by 13-inch baking pan, line it with parchment paper, and grease the paper.

2. In a large mixing bowl, combine the flour, oats, brown sugar, cinnamon, and baking soda. Sprinkle the butter cubes over the dry ingredients and cut them in using a pastry blender, 2 knives, or your fingertips until the dough resembles a crumb topping. Stir in the pecans.

3. Measure out and reserve 1 cup of the pecan crumb mixture. Press the rest into the pan, working it over the bottom in an even layer.

4. Bake the crust for 20 minutes, or until it is an even golden color and slightly firm to the touch. Spread the jam over the warm crust, sprinkle the reserved crumbs over the top, and return the pan to the oven.

5. Bake for about 25 minutes, until the crumbs on top are golden brown and the jam is bubbly. Let cool completely before cutting. To remove the bars from the pan, gently warm the bottom on the stove over low heat and invert onto a cutting board. Remove the paper, place another cutting board over the bar, and invert again. Cut into 2-inch squares.

Photograph on page 187.

VARIATION: APPLE BUTTER WALNUT BARS

Prepare the jam bars as described, substituting a good-quality apple butter for the preserves and walnuts for the pecans.

VICTORY GARDEN CUPCAKES

MAKES 24 STANDARD-SIZE CUPCAKES

Here in the South many of us spend the summer tending to small gardens. Our staff members like to bring in their homegrown vegetables to share. When we have enough, we'll make these decoratively healthy cupcakes filled with carrots, zucchini, and apple, which is an inspired way to utilize the summertime harvest.

1 large tart green apple, peeled and cored

2 medium carrots, peeled

1 small zucchini

1 cup canola or other neutral vegetable oil

1½ cups packed light brown sugar

½ teaspoon salt

3 eggs

2 cups unbleached all-purpose flour

2 teaspoons ground cinnamon

1 teaspoon baking soda

⅔ cup walnut pieces

3 to 4 cups Cream Cheese Frosting (page 70, optional)

1 Preheat the oven to 350°F. Place paper liners in 24 standard-size muffin cups.

2 Using the large holes on a box grater, shred ¾ cup each of the apple, carrots, and zucchini, measuring them firmly packed.

3 In a mixing bowl, whisk the oil with the brown sugar and salt. Add the eggs and whisk until smooth. Sift the flour, cinnamon, and baking soda over the batter; fold a few times to mix partially. Sprinkle the shredded fruit and vegetables over the batter with the walnuts. Fold until the batter is well mixed. Divide among the muffin cups using a ¼-cup measure.

4 Bake for 20 minutes, or until a toothpick or cake tester inserted in the center of a cupcake comes out clean. Let cool in the pans for about 10 minutes, then remove the cupcakes and cool completely on a rack. Ice with cream cheese frosting or serve plain.

Strawberry Cupcakes (top and middle, page 192) and Black Bottom Cupcakes (bottom)

BLACK BOTTOM CUPCAKES

MAKES 12 JUMBO OR 24 STANDARD-SIZE CUPCAKES

When you see how this dessert forms layers—with the very dark cocoa batter sinking to the bottom and the cream cheese filling oozing up in the center—you'll understand where these cupcakes get their name. You can make these killer sweets extra large, like individual cakes, or in regular muffin tins, as ordinary cupcake size—perfect for packing in a lunchbox or as the star offering at your next potluck.

12 ounces cream cheese
(*not* reduced-fat or whipped)

1½ cups plus ⅔ cup sugar

2 large eggs

1 cup mini semisweet chocolate chips

2 cups unbleached all-purpose flour

⅔ cup unsweetened cocoa powder

1¾ teaspoons baking soda

1 teaspoon salt

4 teaspoons distilled white or cider vinegar

1 teaspoon vanilla extract

½ cup canola or other neutral vegetable oil

Baking Tip: Inserting a toothpick won't be an accurate test for doneness with this cupcake since the cream cheese and chocolate chips will remain soft and cause the cupcakes to appear underdone. The best method really is sight and touch.

1 Preheat the oven to 350°F. Place paper liners in 12 jumbo muffin cups or 24 standard-size muffin cups. Place the cream cheese in a mixing bowl and, with the electric mixer on medium-low speed, slowly beat in ⅔ cup of the sugar. Continue to mix until very well blended but do not allow the cream cheese to become too warm and fluffy.

2 Add the eggs, one at a time, mixing until blended and scraping down the bowl well between additions. Fold in the chocolate chips by hand.

3 In a large bowl, sift together the flour, cocoa powder, baking soda, salt, and remaining 1½ cups sugar. Whisk briefly to blend the dry ingredients. Fill a 2-cup measuring cup with 1½ cups water. Add the vinegar and vanilla to the water. Pour all the vegetable oil and half the water mixture into the dry ingredients. Using a whisk, begin blending the batter by hand. Scrape the bowl and add the rest of the water. Whisk until blended, scrape the bowl, and whisk again just until thoroughly mixed.

4 For jumbo cupcakes, scoop ⅓ cup of the chocolate batter into each cup; for standard-size cupcakes, scoop ¼ cup. Top the chocolate batter in the jumbo cups with a scant ¼ cup of the chocolate chip cream cheese; spoon 2 tablespoons onto the standard size.

5 Bake the jumbo cupcakes for about 40 minutes; the standard ones for 30 to 35 minutes. When done, the cake will feel firm around the edges and the cream cheese will be a light golden brown. Let cool in the pans for 10 to 15 minutes, then remove them and cool completely.

STRAWBERRY CUPCAKES

MAKES ABOUT 72 MINI CUPCAKES OR 20 STANDARD-SIZE CUPCAKES

Petits fours are unbelievably popular in the South, but they are a little precious for the Loveless. These mini cupcakes are a good substitute. While diminutive cakes are charming, you can also bake the standard size, which are less time-consuming to make and frost and are guaranteed to be the hit of any kid's birthday party.

2 cups fresh ripe strawberries, stemmed and hulled

2⅓ cups cake flour

1¾ cups sugar

3½ teaspoons baking powder

1½ sticks (6 ounces) unsalted butter, softened

4 egg whites

⅓ cup buttermilk

1 teaspoon vanilla extract

Strawberry Buttercream (recipe follows)

1 Preheat the oven to 350°F. Place paper or foil cupcake liners in 72 mini muffin cups or 20 standard-sized muffin cups.

2 Puree the strawberries in a food processor or blender; measure out ¾ cup for the batter and reserve ¼ cup for the frosting.

3 Combine the cake flour, sugar, and baking powder in a large mixing bowl and with the electric mixer on low, blend to combine, about 20 seconds. Add the softened butter and the strawberry puree and mix on low speed until the dry ingredients are moistened. Raise the speed to medium and mix until light and fluffy, 3 to 5 minutes.

4 In a mixing bowl, whisk together the egg whites, buttermilk, and vanilla. Add the egg white mixture to the flour mixture in several additions, scraping the bowl once or twice and mixing each time only until blended. Spoon 1 tablespoon of the batter into each of the mini cupcake tins or ¼ cup into each standard cup.

5 Bake until a toothpick or cake tester inserted in the center of cupcake comes out clean, 12 to 14 minutes for mini cupcakes, about 20 minutes for standard. Remove the pans from the oven and as soon as the cupcakes can be handled, remove them from the pans, and allow them to cool completely on a rack.

6 To decorate, scoop the strawberry buttercream into a pastry bag with a large open star tip, or use a spreader or an offset spatula to frost the top of each cupcake.

Photograph on page 190.

Strawberry Buttercream

MAKES ABOUT 3 CUPS

3 sticks (12 ounces) unsalted butter, softened

4½ cups confectioners' sugar, sifted

¼ cup fresh strawberry puree (reserved in step 2, opposite)

1½ teaspoons vanilla extract

1. Cream the butter in a large mixing bowl for 1 to 2 minutes, to whip lightly. Add the confectioners' sugar 1 cup at a time and continue beating.

2. Add the strawberry puree and vanilla, scrape the bowl well, and beat until the frosting is light and fluffy, 3 to 5 minutes. Use at once.

Ever since our gift shop, the Loveless Hams & Jams Country Market, opened in 1982, it's been a destination for folks before or after a meal at the cafe or while they're waiting for a table. Southern hams, smoked bacon, mugs, caps, T-shirts, and other souvenir paraphernalia, along with Loveless fruit preserves, biscuit mix, pound cakes, and cookies prove irresistible to most. If you can't get to Tennessee, you can still order from our catalog or the Hams & Jams online store: www.hamsandjams.com.

Puddings

Clockwise from top left: Vanilla Pudding (page 199), Butterscotch Pudding (page 200), and Chocolate Pudding (page 198)

Why are puddings so comforting? Do they simply offer pleasant memories of our younger years, or are they soothing reminders that desserts can be a welcome respite in a complicated world? What we do know is that puddings fit in perfectly with the down-home, casual comfort of the cafe, and our Loveless Banana Pudding remains one of the most popular desserts on our menu.

In fact, few desserts in Tennessee are as ubiquitous as banana pudding. From homes and cafeterias to political back rooms and high-end purveyors of "new" Southern cuisine, it's the dessert against which all personal preferences are measured, and that makes the Loveless Banana Pudding a crowning achievement. Most back-of-the-box recipes use the classic vanilla wafer, a cookie that gained statewide fame in the 1980s along the campaign trail of popular Tennessee governor Ned Ray McWherter. His fondness for the little cookies grew from a lifetime of eating banana pudding, and he employed the image of Nilla wafers with a cup of coffee as all the motivation he needed to get to work sorting out the state's business.

At the Loveless Cafe, we take that dish and dress it up a bit, respectfully replacing the dense wafers with deliciously light ladyfingers. We also use real bananas, and our extra-rich homemade vanilla pudding. Once those flavors get to know each other in the refrigerator overnight, you'll realize why we never skimp on ingredients in any of our recipes.

You'll find more classic Southern pudding recipes here, like butterscotch and tapioca, plus a decadent chocolate bread pudding made with brownies. However, our most interesting variation, Biscuit Pudding with Drunken Caramel Sauce, will come as no surprise to anyone who has ever eaten at the Loveless. For a place rightfully famous for biscuits, it just wouldn't be right not to incorporate them into a sweet creation, adding an exclamation point to an iconic food that has defined Loveless comfort for more than sixty years.

CHOCOLATE PUDDING

SERVES 4

Just a few ingredients and ten minutes at most yield a perfectly delicious homemade pudding. With all the chocolates available now, you can create a different pudding each time you make it. For a less intense chocolate flavor, try a semisweet chocolate; for a more sophisticated taste, use a bittersweet chocolate that's high in cacao. Children often prefer pudding made with milk chocolate.

2 cups half-and-half

⅔ cup sugar

2 tablespoons cornstarch

4 egg yolks, at room temperature

2 ounces unsweetened chocolate, chopped into small pieces

1 In a small heavy saucepan, combine 1¾ cups of the half-and-half and the sugar. Slowly bring to a boil over medium-low heat, stirring to dissolve the sugar.

2 Place the cornstarch in a heatproof bowl. Whisk in the remaining ¼ cup half-and-half to make a smooth paste. Add the egg yolks and whisk until blended. To temper the egg yolks, gradually whisk in about one-third of the hot half-and-half in a thin stream to warm them. Slowly whisk the warmed egg yolk mixture back into the remaining half-and-half in the saucepan. Return to a boil over medium-low heat, whisking constantly; continue to boil, whisking, for 1 minute.

3 Remove the pan from the heat and add the chocolate. Whisk gently until the chocolate is melted and smooth, making sure to scrape down the sides of the pan so that no streaks remain. Strain the pudding into a serving bowl or 4 dessert dishes. Cover with plastic wrap, pressing it right onto the surface to prevent a skin from forming. Refrigerate the pudding for 2 to 4 hours, until completely chilled, before serving.

Photograph on page 195.

Baking Tip: Even though the egg yolks in a stirred pudding are tempered by gradual warming to produce a silky smooth dessert, the cornstarch used as a thickener protects them from curdling. That's why a pudding can be boiled to finish cooking at the end without any worry.

VANILLA PUDDING

SERVES 4

With an intense vanilla flavor from the bean that is steeped in the cream, this pudding can be served by itself in a fancy glass cup, as we do at the Loveless, perhaps with a cookie or two, or used as a component of another, more complex dessert. Fresh fruit tarts and trifles come to mind; so do cream puffs. Because this pudding is made with half-and-half rather than milk, it has a richness and body that make it a real treat.

2 cups half-and-half

¼ cup sugar

¼ vanilla bean, split lengthwise in half

2 tablespoons plus 2 teaspoons cornstarch

4 egg yolks, at room temperature

1. In a small saucepan, combine 1¾ cups of the half-and-half and the sugar. Scrape the seeds from the vanilla bean into the pan with the tip of a knife and add the pod as well. Bring to a boil over medium-low heat, stirring occasionally to dissolve the sugar. Remove from the heat and keep warm.

2. Place the cornstarch in a small heatproof bowl. Whisk in the remaining ¼ cup half-and-half to make a smooth paste. Whisk in the egg yolks. To temper the egg yolks, slowly whisk in about one-third of the hot half-and-half in a thin stream. Whisk the egg yolk mixture back into the remaining half-and-half in the saucepan. Return to medium-low heat and return to a boil, whisking constantly. Boil, whisking, for 1 minute to cook the cornstarch.

3. Strain the pudding into a serving bowl or 4 dessert dishes; discard the vanilla pod. Cover with plastic wrap, pressing it right onto the surface to prevent a skin from forming. Refrigerate the pudding for 2 to 4 hours, until completely chilled, before serving.

Photograph on page 195.

BUTTERSCOTCH PUDDING

SERVES 4

Real butterscotch flavor is complex: buttery with a hint of caramel, salty, and sweet all at the same time. Making stirred pudding like this is much easier than you'd expect, because you don't have to worry about the egg yolks curdling. The only tricky part is caramelizing the brown sugar without burning it.

⅔ cup packed dark brown sugar

1 inch of vanilla bean, split lengthwise in half

2 cups half-and-half

½ teaspoon kosher salt

3 tablespoons cornstarch

4 egg yolks, at room temperature

3 tablespoons unsalted butter, softened

1 tablespoon plus 1 teaspoon dark rum

1. To make the caramel, place the brown sugar in a deep heavy saucepan and stir in 3 tablespoons water. Set over medium-low heat and bring to a simmer, stirring to dissolve the sugar. As soon as the syrup starts to boil, place a candy thermometer in the pot and cook without stirring until it reaches 255°F. Immediately remove from the heat.

2. With the tip of a knife, scrape the seeds of the vanilla bean into a small saucepan and toss in the pod. Add 1¾ cups of the half-and-half and the salt and warm over low heat.

3. When the caramel reaches 255°F, quickly whisk in ½ cup of the hot half-and-half. Whisk in the warm half-and-half in several more additions until it is all incorporated. Return the caramel cream to medium-low heat and bring to a boil, whisking gently and scraping the bottom of the pan. Remove the caramel cream from the heat. Discard the vanilla bean.

4. In a heatproof bowl, mix the remaining ¼ cup half-and-half and the cornstarch, whisking until smooth. Add the egg yolks and whisk until blended. To temper the egg yolks, slowly whisk in about one-third of the caramel cream in a thin stream. Whisk the warmed egg yolks back into the remaining caramel cream in the saucepan and bring to a boil over medium-low heat, whisking constantly. Cook, whisking, for 1 minute.

5. Remove from the heat and stir in the butter and rum. Discard the vanilla pod. Strain the pudding into a large serving bowl or 4 individual dessert dishes. Cover with plastic wrap, pressing it right onto the surface to prevent a skin from forming. Refrigerate until completely chilled before serving, 2 to 4 hours.

Photograph on page 195.

TAPIOCA PUDDING

SERVES 4

Half-and-half, vanilla bean, and just a touch of nutmeg kick this homey dessert up a notch. Serve it plain or layer with fruit for a tapioca parfait.

2½ cups half-and-half

⅔ cup sugar

2 tablespoons plus 1 teaspoon quick-cooking tapioca

1 inch of vanilla bean, split lengthwise in half

2 egg yolks, at room temperature

Freshly grated nutmeg for garnish

1 Place the half-and-half, sugar, and tapioca in a heavy medium saucepan. With the tip of a knife, scrape the seeds of the vanilla bean into the pan and toss in the pod. Let stand for 15 minutes to soften the tapioca. Turn the heat to medium-low and cook, stirring frequently, until the tapioca pearls are translucent and the mixture is slightly thickened, 10 to 12 minutes.

2 Place the egg yolks in a heatproof bowl and whisk lightly. To temper them, gradually whisk in about half of the hot pudding. Gradually stir this mixture into the remaining tapioca in the pan and cook over medium-low heat, stirring constantly, until the pudding thickens, 10 to 12 minutes; do not boil. Discard the vanilla pod.

3 Immediately divide the pudding among 4 small serving dishes or pour into one larger bowl. Cover with plastic wrap, pressing it right onto the surface to prevent a skin from forming. Refrigerate until chilled and set, 2 to 4 hours or overnight. Serve cold, dusted with a pinch of nutmeg.

LOVELESS BANANA PUDDING

SERVES 6 TO 8

No dessert is more Southern than banana pudding, and this one is as easy as it comes. At the cafe, we make a big batch to scoop out home style with a spoon. Real pudding made from scratch in less than 15 minutes and purchased ladyfingers—a tad more sophisticated than the usual vanilla wafers—make an everyday dessert special enough for company.

⅓ cup cornstarch

3 cups whole milk

8 egg yolks, at room temperature

¾ cup plus 1 tablespoon sugar

1 inch of vanilla bean, split lengthwise in half

4 to 6 bananas, ripened but not bruised or blemished, sliced

About 24 ladyfingers, boudoir biscuits, or savoiardi

1 cup heavy cream

1. To make the pudding, place the cornstarch in a heatproof bowl. Stir in ½ cup of the milk until evenly blended. Whisk in the egg yolks.

2. Combine the remaining 2½ cups milk and ¾ cup of the sugar in a heavy medium saucepan. With the tip of a knife, scrape the vanilla seeds into the pan; toss in the pod as well. Bring to a boil over medium heat; immediately reduce the heat to low.

3. Slowly whisk about half of the hot milk into the egg yolk mixture to warm it. Then whisk the hot egg mixture into the remaining milk in a slow, steady stream. Continue to cook, whisking, until the pudding comes to a gentle boil. Boil for a minute, remove the vanilla pod, remove from the heat, and scrape into a bowl. Press a sheet of plastic wrap directly onto the top of the pudding to prevent a skin from forming; refrigerate until cold, at least 4 hours or overnight.

4. To assemble the dessert, spread a thin layer of chilled pudding in a trifle dish or other deep glass or ceramic bowl. Top with a layer of overlapping banana slices and then a layer of ladyfingers. Cover with half of the remaining pudding, another layer of bananas, reserving a few slices for garnish, and then the rest of the ladyfingers, reserving 2 or 3 for garnish. Top with the remaining pudding. Cover with plastic wrap and refrigerate for at least 6 hours or up to a day in advance before serving so the cookies soften completely.

5 Shortly before serving, whip the cream and the remaining 1 tablespoon sugar in a chilled bowl with chilled beaters until soft peaks form. Top the banana pudding with dollops of whipped cream, a sprinkling of the reserved ladyfingers, crumbled, and a few slices of banana.

BISCUIT PUDDING
WITH DRUNKEN CARAMEL SAUCE

SERVES 8

When the Loveless Cafe closes at the end of the day, there are usually some biscuits lying around. That's because it's Loveless policy never to run out; so up until closing, guests have a chance to eat their fill—fresh and hot. Consequently, when we finally close our doors, there are almost always some left over. Rather than toss them, we use them to make biscuit bread pudding, which is served warm the next day with a drizzle of caramel sauce. You can make this dessert with any leftover biscuits, homemade or store-bought.

1/3 cup raisins

16 cold 2-inch biscuits

4 eggs

3/4 cup sugar

2 cups half-and-half

1 1/2 teaspoons vanilla extract

Drunken Caramel Sauce (page 206)

Buttermilk or vanilla ice cream (optional)

1 Place the raisins in a small saucepan and cover them with water. Bring to a gentle boil over low heat. Boil for a minute or two; then remove from the heat and let the raisins cool to room temperature to plump them.

2 Crumble the biscuits. Grease an 11 by 7-inch glass or ceramic baking dish and spread the crumbled biscuits evenly over the bottom. Drain the raisins and sprinkle over the biscuits.

3 In a mixing bowl, whisk the eggs with the sugar until blended. Add the half-and-half and vanilla and mix well. Pour this custard over the biscuits, cover with foil, and let stand for 15 to 20 minutes.

4 Meanwhile, preheat the oven to 350°F. Bake the foil-covered bread pudding for 1 hour and 10 minutes, or until the custard is set. Remove from the oven and let stand, uncovered, for 10 to 15 minutes. Cut the pudding into 8 pieces and serve each warm with a drizzle of the caramel sauce and, if you are feeling especially decadent, a scoop of ice cream.

Drunken Caramel Sauce

MAKES ABOUT 1¼ CUPS

1/3 cup heavy cream

1 tablespoon unsalted butter

1 small cinnamon stick

1 inch of vanilla bean, split lengthwise in half

1 cup sugar

2 tablespoons light corn syrup

1/4 cup bourbon, whiskey, or dark rum

1 In a small saucepan, combine the cream, butter, and cinnamon stick. Scrape the seeds from the vanilla bean into the pan using the tip of a knife and toss in the pod. Set over low heat to warm the cream, melt the butter, and infuse the flavors, about 3 minutes.

2 In a separate deep saucepan, combine the sugar, corn syrup, and 1/4 cup water. Bring to a boil over medium-low heat, stirring to melt the sugar. Using a moist brush, wash any sugar crystals off the sides of the pan. Continue to boil without stirring until the sugar syrup begins to color. Once it turns golden, gently swirl the pan and watch it closely. As soon as the caramel turns an even amber shade, remove from the heat.

3 Carefully pour a few tablespoons of the warm cream into the caramel; the mixture will boil up furiously. Whisk until smooth. Slowly whisk in the remaining cream. Continue to whisk until all the caramel is dissolved. Stir in the bourbon, remove the vanilla pod, and let the sauce cool to room temperature before serving.

It's difficult to choose favorites from the pie case at the front of the cafe, but undoubtedly Double-Coconut Cream Pie and Muddy Fudge Pie are our best sellers, followed closely by Chocolate Cookie–Peanut Butter Pie, and specialty pies like our signature Loveless Steeplechase Pie and Turtle Pie.

RICE PUDDING

SERVES 4 TO 6

When we first reopened the Loveless after major renovations, we added rice pudding to the dessert menu. A wonderful creamy rice pudding is best made with basmati rice, whose nuttiness adds a dimension of flavor that plain long-grain rice just doesn't have.

3 cups whole milk

½ cup long-grain white rice, preferably basmati

1 small cinnamon stick

¼ vanilla bean, split lengthwise in half

½ cup granulated sugar

4 egg yolks, at room temperature

Cinnamon sugar and whipped cream for garnish

1 Place the milk, rice, and cinnamon stick in a heavy medium saucepan. With the tip of a knife, scrape the seeds from the vanilla bean into the pan and toss in the pod. Bring to a simmer over medium-low heat, reduce the heat to low, and cook gently, uncovered, stirring frequently to prevent sticking, until the rice is very soft, 30 to 40 minutes; the pudding will still look very liquid. Remove the vanilla pod and cinnamon stick. Add the granulated sugar and return to a simmer, stirring to dissolve the sugar.

2 To temper the egg yolks, place them in a heatproof bowl and whisk lightly. Then very gradually whisk about one-third of the hot rice pudding into the yolks. Return the remaining rice pudding to a boil, reduce the heat to low, and whisk in the warmed egg yolk mixture. Cook just below a simmer, stirring often, until slightly thickened, 2 to 3 minutes; do not allow to boil or the yolks will curdle.

3 Immediately pour the pudding into a bowl. Serve warm or slightly chilled. Garnish with a sprinkle of cinnamon sugar and whipped cream.

Baking Tip: You'll notice one thing missing in this recipe: raisins. That's because we've learned that people who like them will eat rice pudding either way, but people who don't won't eat pudding with raisins in it. If you do want to add them, there's one rule you should always follow: Plump them in boiling water first. Otherwise they can draw out moisture and make the rice pudding dry.

BROWNIE BREAD PUDDING

SERVES 8

Catering requests at the Loveless Barn invariably include chocolate bread pudding. The problem with adding chocolate to the kind of thin custard used for bread pudding is that the ingredients often separate into layers, with the chocolate settling at the bottom and a paler, less flavorful custard migrating to the top. Usual remedies for this are time-consuming, so we use some leftover but perfectly good brownies as the base instead. They sop up the vanilla custard and result in the perfect chocolate "bread" pudding.

Double-Chocolate Fudge Brownies (page 177), made 1 day ahead with 2 extra tablespoons flour to equal 1 cup

5 eggs

²/₃ cup sugar

2¹/₂ cups half-and-half

1¹/₂ teaspoons vanilla extract

Drunken Caramel Sauce (page 206)

Vanilla ice cream (optional)

1 Crumble the day-old brownies into a shallow bowl and let sit out overnight, uncovered, to dry out a bit. If the brownies are stale already, you may be able to skip this step.

2 Preheat the oven to 375°F. Grease a 7 by 11-inch baking dish and spread the crumbled brownies evenly over the bottom. In a mixing bowl, whisk the eggs with the sugar until blended. Mix in the half-and-half and vanilla. Pour over the brownies, cover with foil, and let stand for 15 to 20 minutes to give the brownie crumbs time to absorb the custard.

3 Bake the foil-covered brownies for about 1 hour, until the custard is set. Remove from the oven and let stand for about 15 minutes. Cut the pudding into 8 pieces and serve warm with a drizzle of the caramel sauce and a scoop of vanilla ice cream, if you wish.

Sources

Use the following sources to order specialty ingredients online.

CARAMEL, *CAJETA,* AND *DULCE DE LECHE*
Mex Grocer:
www.mexgrocer.com/brand-coronado
.html
Also available in Latino markets and international markets

CRYSTAL SUGAR
India Tree: www.indiatree.com
King Arthur Flour:
www.kingarthurflour.com
Wilton: www.wilton.com

GRANOLA
Loveless Homemade Granola:
www.lovelesscafe.com

HONEY AND SORGHUM
Loveless Cafe Honey and Sorghum:
www.lovelesscafe.com

KEY LIME JUICE
Nellie & Joe's: www.keylimejuice.com
Also available in many supermarkets

ROOT BEER
Natural Brew Root Beer:
www.natural-brew.com/products/
draft_root_beer
Also available in Whole Foods Markets

ROSE WATER
King Arthur Flour:
www.kingarthurflour.com
Also available in Middle Eastern markets and Indian groceries

SELF-RISING FLOUR
White Lily: www.whitelily.com

VANILLA BEANS
Amadeus Vanilla Beans:
www.amadeusvanillabeans.com/store
Beanilla: www.beanilla.com/index.php
Nielsen Massey: www.nielsenmassey.com
Also available at Whole Foods Markets and Williams-Sonoma

Bibliography

The following books were used for inspiration and information and were enormously helpful in writing this cookbook.

Berolzheimer, Ruth, ed. *The American Woman's Cook Book, Wartime Edition*. Chicago: Consolidated Book Publishers, 1944.

Choate, Judith. *The Great American Pie Book*. New York: Simon & Schuster, 1992.

Choice Recipes from Choices Restaurant. Franklin, Tenn.: Choices Restaurant, 1991.

Claire, Mabel. *Macy's Cook Book and Kitchen Guide for the Busy Woman*. New York: Greenberg Publisher, 1932.

Dupree, Nathalie. *Nathalie Dupree's Southern Memories*. Athens: University of Georgia Press, 2004.

Glenn, Camille. *The Heritage of Southern Cooking*. New York: Workman, 1986.

Hilburn, Prudence. *A Treasury of Southern Baking*. New York: HarperCollins, 1993.

Hunter, Ethel Farmer. *Secrets of Southern Cooking*. New York: Tudor Publishing Company, 1956.

King, Daisy. *Recipes from Miss Daisy's*. Nashville: Rutledge Hill Press, 1985.

Lewis, Edna, and Scott Peacock. *The Gift of Southern Cooking*. New York: Alfred A. Knopf, 2003.

Nashville Area Home Economics Association. *The Nashville Cookbook*. Nashville: 1976.

Sax, Richard. *Classic Home Desserts*. Shelburne, Vt.: Chapters Publishing, 1994.

Scott, Pearlie B. *Tennessee Treasure*. Nashville: Williams Printing Company, 1985.

Acknowledgments

While working on this book, I asked many people questions about their favorite desserts. More than a few offered stories as well as recipes. One person who shared stories and thoughts was Carol Fay Ellison, the Loveless Cafe's "Biscuit Lady." She and I had many conversations about her aunt Hazel's legendary desserts. More than once, Carol Fay helped me get a recipe "just right" by describing how Aunt Hazel had prepared it. Other times, she simply told me what something "should" have in it, as she did when she talked to me about buttermilk and chess pies. I can still hear her asking "Got meal in it?" Mostly, she would taste and offer either her opinion or her approval, sometimes both. She passed away before I completed this book, so I never had the chance to share it with her or thank her for her support and friendship.

To Tom Morales, for giving me this opportunity, and to Jesse Goldstein, for his never-ending enthusiasm and support. Honestly, without either of them, this book would not have been possible.

All of my coworkers at the Loveless Cafe tasted an endless array of desserts while I worked out kinks in the recipes; I truly appreciate their support and their honesty. To everyone who shared recipes and memories, I offer my heartfelt thanks.

Six unbelievably hot days and dozens upon dozens of freshly baked desserts resulted in the amazing photos, thanks to Jan Derevjanik, one incredible art director, and intrepid photographer Karen Mordechai.

To Sheila B, whose ability to turn doors into tables and to find absolutely everything we needed went well beyond the call of duty. I cannot thank her enough.

Many, many thanks to Ann Bramson, Judy Pray, and the entire Artisan staff for working so hard on this book. To Susan Wyler, for believing in me and this project.

To my mother, Carol Truglio, for her spice cookies and fried bows. To my grandmother Virginia Truglio for sharing her love of sweets. And to my great-grandmother Frances Paulillo for the many bowls of Jell-O during my early childhood.

Last but not least, to my own little family: Darry, Alix, and Devon. Their love and support mean the world to me.

Index

Note: Page references in italics refer to photographs.